NICOTEXT

BLA BLA

Fredrik Colting
Carl-Johan Gadd
Edited by: Lara Allen

www.nicotext.com
info@nicotext.com

Printed in Canada

ISBN 91-974882-1-6

ALL FACTS IN THIS BOOK ARE ABSOLUTELY,
AND WITHOUT A DOUBT TRUE.
IN THE SECRET LABORATORIES OF NICOTEXT,
JUST OUTSIDE GENEVA, MYSTICAL SCIENTISTS
IN BLACK SUITS SCIENTIFICALLY TESTED
THESE FACTS.

IF SOMETHING IN THIS BOOK, CONTRARY
TO OUR EXPECTATIONS, TURNS OUT TO
BE FALSE, NICOTEXT'S ASTUTE SCIENTISTS
WILL OF COURSE RECEIVE THE HONOUR
OF BRINGING FORTH THEIR SCIENTIFIC DATA
ON THE SUBJECT IN QUESTION.

SO, TO ALL OF YOU SAYING "HMMM"...
CAN THIS REALLY BE TRUE?

YES, IT CAN!

**THE WALKMAN WAS FIRST
INTRODUCED IN 1979.**

**THE FIRST OWNER OF THE MARLBORO
COMPANY DIED OF LUNG CANCER.**

**THERE ARE MORE THAN 500 GIVEN
PHOBIAS. ONE OF THE RAREST IS
HOPLOPHOBIA –
A FEAR OF FIRE TRUCKS.**

THERE ARE MORE THAN 17,000 AIRPLANES IN THE WORLD, OF WHICH 4,000 ARE ALWAYS AIRBORNE.

90 % OF THE CAB DRIVERS IN NEW YORK ARE RECENTLY LANDED IMMIGRANTS.

MADAGASCAR, OUTSIDE THE EASTERN COAST OF AFRICA, IS THE FOURTH LARGEST ISLAND IN THE WORLD.

CHARLES BRONSON'S GIVEN NAME
AT BIRTH WAS CHARLES BUCHINSKY.
ERIC CLAPTON'S WAS PATRICK CLAPP.

THE WORD "AMATEUR" COMES FROM
THE SAME SPELLED FRENCH WORD
FOR "LOVER" AND
"IS ANYONE INTERESTED?"

35% OF ALL ADVERTISERS IN
PERSONAL ADS ARE ALREADY
MARRIED.

UNTIL THE BEGINNING OF THE 20TH CENTURY, PURE COCAINE WAS SOLD AT HARROD'S IN LONDON, ENGLAND.

IF YOU ORDER VIKIN-RYORI IN JAPAN, YOU CAN PICK FOOD FROM A SMORGASBORD.

REMBRANDT'S GRANDFATHER WAS A BAKER.

THE LEGENDARY CLASSIC FILM
COMEDIAN HARPO MARX, ALONG
WITH HIS CHATTY BROTHERS,
BECAME FAMOUS BY NOT SPEAKING
A SINGLE WORD ON SCREEN.
IN REAL LIFE, HE HAD NO TROUBLE
UTTERING THE SPOKEN WORD.

LONDON ENGLAND'S CLOCKWORK IS
LOCATED ON THE CLOCK TOWER OF
WESTMINSTER BRIDGE. IT IS ALSO
KNOWN AS BIG BEN AND FOR
KEEPING THE EXACT TIME.
IN 1945, HOWEVER, IT SLOWED DOWN
BY FIVE MINUTES DUE TO A FLOCK
OF STARLINGS SITTING ON THE
MINUTE HAND.

THERE ARE TRAFFIC LIGHTS ON THE CANALS IN VENICE.

THE WORD SCHOOL COMES FROM THE GREEK WORD SKHOL, WHICH MEANS LEISURE TIME, TIME FOR SPIRITUAL EXERCISES.

IN THE AMERICAN CITY OF MONTPELIER, A CONTEST IS HELD YEARLY TO DETERMINE WHO HAS THE MOST WORN OUT PAIR OF SNEAKERS. THE CONTEST IS CALLED *THE ANNUAL INTERNATIONAL ROTTEN SNEAKER CONTEST.*

THE METALLIC ELEMENT GALLIUM
HAS MOST PECULIAR PROPERTIES.
IF YOU PUT A PIECE OF THE METAL
IN YOUR HAND, IT WILL MELT.
THE MELTING POINT OF THE METAL IS
29.76 DEGREES CELSIUS, (85.312°F).

AN ELK HAS FOUR STOMACHS.

ALFRED HITCHCOCK MADE IT A
GIMMICK BY HAVING A CAMEO IN HIS
OWN MOVIES FOR A FEW SECONDS.
HOWEVER, IN 25 OF HIS MOVIES YOU
CAN'T SEE HIM.

**A RAT'S TEETH GROW ABOUT
6 INCHES IN A YEAR.**

**ADOLF HITLER WAS BORN IN
AUSTRIA BUT MOVED TO GERMANY
TO AVOID BEING CALLED FOR
MILITARY SERVICE.**

**THE JAPANESE NATIONAL ANTHEM IS
THE OLDEST ANTHEM IN
THE WORLD.**

A CROCODILE CAN'T
STICK ITS TONGUE OUT.

DURING AN ORDINARY DAY, YOUR
HAND WILL INDIRECTLY COME IN
CONTACT WITH 15 PENISES.

STEVIE WONDER MADE HIS RECORD
DEBUT WHEN HE WAS JUST
12 YEARS OLD.

HOLLAND AND THE NETHERLANDS ARE NOT ONE IN THE SAME. SINCE THE 16TH CENTURY, THE NAME OF THE NATION HAS BEEN THE NETHERLANDS. HOLLAND CONSISTS OF TWO PROVINCES THAT TOGETHER ONLY COVER ONE SIXTH OF THE AREA OF THE NETHERLANDS.

A COW BURPS EVERY 40 SECONDS.

BEFORE THEY CHANGED THEIR NAMES, DEMI MOORE WAS CALLED DEMETRIA GUYNES, AND WALTHER MATTHAU WAS CALLED WALTER MATUSHANSKATASKY.

THE AVERAGE AGE FOR A PORSCHE OWNER IS 49 WHILE THAT OF A HARLEY DAVIDSON OWNER IS 52.

THE AUSTRALIAN ABORIGINALS HAVE MORE TEETH THAN OTHER HUMAN BEINGS.

IN FAIRBANKS, ALASKA A LAW FORBID ELKS TO HAVE SEX ON THE STREETS.

**THE AVERAGE MAN WILL HAVE
ABOUT 7,200 ORGASMS
IN A LIFETIME.**

**THE AVERAGE SPEED OF A
MAN'S ORGASM IS 28 MPH.**

WHALES HAVE NO VOCAL CORDS.

**ONLY 55% OF ALL AMERICANS KNOW
THAT THE SUN IS A STAR.**

JAMES DEAN'S REAL NAME WAS
JAMES BYRON, AND WHOOPI
GOLDBERG WAS BORN
CARYN JOHNSON.

THE ODDS OF DYING WHILE FALLING
OUT OF BED ARE 1 IN 2 MILLION.

ON AVERAGE, EVERY PERSON
WILL SWALLOW THREE SPIDERS
EACH YEAR.

WHEN EINSTEIN WAS NINE YEARS OLD, HE COULD NOT SPEAK PROPERLY. HIS PARENTS SUSPECTED THAT HE WAS MENTALLY RETARDED.

MOST COLLECT CALLS ARE MADE ON FATHER'S DAY.

GEORGE WASHINGTON GREW MARIJUANA IN HIS GARDEN.

IF YOU SPEND ONE HOUR IN A
PUBLIC SWIMMING POOL, YOU
WILL COME IN CONTACT WITH
ABOUT 50 OUNCES OF URINE.

MORE THAN 110 BILLION
TAMPONS HAVE BEEN
SOLD SINCE 1936.

IF YOU ARE EXTREMELY AFRAID
OF MEN, YOU MAY BE SUFFERING
FROM ANDROPHOBIA.

IN ONE YEAR, YOU WILL SWALLOW
14 BUGS IN YOUR SLEEP.

EACH YEAR YOU WILL SHAKE HANDS
WITH 11 WOMEN WHO RECENTLY HAVE
MASTURBATED WITHOUT WASHING
THEIR HANDS AFTERWARDS.

DURING A LIFETIME, 22 CONTRACTED
WORKERS (CARPENTERS,
ELECTRICIANS, ETC.) WILL HAVE
SNOOPED THROUGH THE CONTENTS
OF YOUR LAUNDRY HAMPER.

EVERY DAY, YOU INHALE ABOUT 61 CUBIC INCHES OF OTHER PEOPLES' FARTS.

A RAT CAN LIVE LONGER WITHOUT WATER THAN A CAMEL CAN.

THE MOST COMMON NAME IN THE WORLD IS MOHAMMED.

**THE AVERAGE MAN EATS
110,000 POUNDS OF FOOD
DURING HIS LIFETIME.**

**MOST PEOPLE FALL ASLEEP
WITHIN 7 MINUTES.**

**DURING A SPACE TRIP, IT WAS
DISCOVERED THAT FROGS ARE ABLE
TO THROW UP. FIRST, THE FROG WILL
THROW UP ITS STOMACH, SO THAT IT
HANGS OUT OF ITS MOUTH. NEXT,
WITH ITS FRONT LEGS, THE FROG WILL
REMOVE THE STOMACH CONTENTS.
WHEN FINISHED, IT SWALLOWS THE
STOMACH PUTTING IT BACK IN PLACE.**

THE HUMAN BODY CONTAINS ENOUGH
FAT TO MAKE SEVEN BARS OF SOAP
AND ENOUGH IRON TO MAKE ONE
SEVEN INCH NAIL.

26 ASTRONAUTS HAVE REPORTED
SEEING UFOS WHILE CIRCLING
AROUND THE EARTH.

YOUR BRAIN USES 10 TIMES
MORE OXYGEN THAN THE
REST OF YOUR BODY.

A CAUCASIAN MALE'S RIGHT
TESTICLE WEIGHS TWICE AS MUCH
AS THAT OF AN ASIAN MALE WHICH
AVERAGES 0.35 OUNCES.

THE BAT IS THE ONLY
MAMMAL THAT CAN FLY.

LORD NELSON WAS MISSING
TWO BODY PARTS - ONE LEG
AND ONE EYE.

THE "BIG KAHUNA BURGER" WAS NOT ONLY EATING IN *PULP FICTION*. IT WAS ALSO CONSUMED IN TWO OF QUENTIN TARANTINO'S OTHER MOVIES, *FROM DUSK TILL DAWN* AND *RESERVOIR DOGS*.

SOME HENS PRODUCE GREEN EGGS.

THERE ARE NO FISH IN THE DEAD SEA.

IT WAS PASTA THAT BROUGHT FORTH THE INVENTION OF THE DINNER FORK. FOR HUNDREDS OF YEARS, PEOPLE IN NAPLES ATE THEIR MACARONI WITH THEIR FINGERS. HOWEVER, IT WAS CONSIDERED BAD MANNERS FOR ROYALTY TO EAT THIS WAY WHILE WEARING GOLDEN KNITTED SILK DRESSES IN THE ROYAL COURT.

KING FERDINAND OF SPAIN WELCOMED THE INVENTION OF THE FORK AS IT SUPPORTED HIS FONDNESS FOR MACARONI.

THE WAR BETWEEN ENGLAND AND FRANCE, CALLED "THE HUNDRED YEAR WAR" WENT ON BETWEEN 1337 AND 1453, WHICH MEANS THAT IT ACTUALLY LASTED FOR 116 YEARS!

VINCENT VAN GOGH AND PAUL GAUGUIN SHARED A STUDIO FOR NINE WEEKS. THE TWO ARTISTS OFTEN HAD FIGHTS WITH EACH OTHER AND, DURING A MAD MOMENT, VAN GOGH CUT A PIECE OF HIS OWN LEFT EAR OFF.

IF YOU SUFFER FROM ONOMATOPHOBIA, YOU ARE ENORMOUSLY SCARED OF HEARING CERTAIN NAMES OR WORDS.

RECYCLING IS VERY POPULAR IN THE MOVIE INDUSTRY. FOR EXAMPLE, THE SET FROM THE AXIS CHEMICAL INDUSTRY IN *BATMAN* WERE REMAINS PREVIOUSLY USED IN THE CLASSIC MOVIE *ALIEN*. ROOFTOP SCENERY AND BUILDINGS IN *MATRIX* WERE USED A YEAR EARLIER IN *DARK CITY*.

THE LONGEST ESCALATOR IN THE
WORLD CAN BE FOUND IN
ST. PETERSBURG, RUSSIA – 729
STEPS BRING THE TRAVELLER MORE
THAN 64.5 YARDS UP OR DOWN.

SOME PLANTS IN THE MISTLETOE
FAMILY EMPLOY A UNUSUAL
METHOD FOR SPREADING THEIR
SEEDS. WHEN READY, THE PLANT
EXPLODES AND SHOOTS ITS SEEDS
OFF IN ALL DIRECTIONS AT A SPEED
OF 30 MPH.

THE ABBREVIATION "EEG" STANDS
FOR "ELECTROENCEPHALOGRAPHY"

ORIGINALLY, QUENTIN TARANTINO
WROTE MISTER PINK'S ROLE IN
RESERVOIR DOGS FOR HIMSELF.
IN THE END, STEVE BUSCEMI PLAYED
THE PART.

IN FRANCE, WALKIE TALKIE
IS CALLED TALKIE WALKIE
AND AIDS IS CALLED SIDA.

THE RED CIRCLE ON THE JAPANESE
FLAG SYMBOLISES THE RISING SUN.

VINCENT VAN GOGH CREATED OVER 800 PAINTINGS AND 700 SKETCHES YET ONLY SUCCEDED IN SELLING ONE PAINTING IN HIS THOUGH LIFETIME.

IN 1970, SOVIET SCIENTISTS TRIED TO TRAIN CATS TO CONTROL ROBOTS. THE ATTEMPT FAILED.

EVERY YEAR IN THE USA 13 PEOPLE DIE FROM FALLING VENDING MACHINES.

AN ELEPHANT'S BRAIN IS FIVE TIMES LARGER THAN A HUMAN BRAIN.

EGYPTIAN MUMMIES WERE NOT ORIGINALLY EMBALMED. THEY WERE LAID OUT ON THE HOT DESERT SAND TO DRY WITHOUT ROTTING.

WHALES CAN HAVE LICE.

PETROLEUM IS COLORLESS. RED DYE IS ADDED SO NOT TO CONFUSE IT WITH OTHER FUELS.

THE FIRST MASSAGE DEVICE WAS INVENTED IN 1869 AND POWERED BY STEAM.

ACCORDING TO AN INVESTIGATION, HALF OF ALL MEN RAISED ON A FARM HAVE HAD SEXUAL CONTACT WITH ANIMALS.

PEANUTS ARE NOT NUTS AT ALL, THEY'RE PEAS.

THE HITCHHIKERS GUIDE TO THE GALAXY **BY DOUGLAS ADAMS WAS FIRST RELEASED AS A RADIO SERIES THEN A BOOK.**

ON A HOT DAY, UP TO TEN TONS OF WATER CAN EVAPORATE FROM THE LEAVES OF A LARGE TREE.

YOU SUFFER FROM DENDROPHOBIA IF YOU DON'T LIKE TO BE NEAR TREES OR ARE DEADLY AFRAID OF THEM.

A BABY'S CRY CAN REACH 90 DECIBELS. A NORMAL CONVERSATION MEASURES AROUND 60 DECIBELS AND A CAR HORN 110 DECIBELS.

DO YOU GET HEADACHES WHEN EATING ICE CREAM? ONE THIRD OF THE WORLD'S POPULATION SUFFER FROM IT. IT'S CALLED "SPHENO PALATINE GANGLEONEURALGIA."

THE GREAT WHITE WHALE IN *MOBY DICK* BY HERMAN MEVILLE WAS IN FACT A SPERM WHALE.

TWO MILLION MITES LIVE IN YOUR BED.

WHEN STEVE BUSCHEMI PLAYED MASS MURDERER, GARLAND GREEN, IN THE MOVIE *CONAIR*, HE ASKED THE DIRECTOR WHETHER OR NOT HE NEEDED A WIG OR ANY SPECIFIC MAKEUP TO MAKE HIM LOOK SCARIER. THE DIRECTOR TOLD HIM IT WOULD BE ENOUGH TO JUST LOOK LIKE HIMSELF.

IN 1994, 36,021 WRONGLY PARKED
CARS WERE TOWED AWAY IN
NEW YORK CITY.

TOM HANKS, WHO PLAYED THE LEAD
CHARACTER IN *FORREST GUMP* HAS
HIS EYES CLOSED IN EVERY STILL
PHOTO SHOWN IN THE MOVIE OF
FORREST'S LIFE.

A LIGHTNING BOLT IS NOT VERY WIDE
– USUALLY BETWEEN 1 TO 2 INCHES
BUT IT CAN BE UP TO 6 INCHES IN
WIDTH. ITS LENGTH IS MUCH MORE
DAZZLING – OFTEN BETWEEN 328
YARDS AND 2 MILES LONG.

PASTA MEANS DOUGH IN ITALIAN.

A MORE FITTING WORD FOR WRITER'S CRAMP IS "MIGIOGRAPHY".

THE PRODUCERS, OF THE FILM *SEVEN*, WANTED KEVIN SPACEY'S NAME AMONG THE CREDITS AT THE BEGINNING OF THE MOVIE. BUT SPACEY DIDN'T WANT THIS. HE WANTED TO SURPRISE THE AUDIENCE AND NOT GIVE AWAY THAT FACT THAT HE WAS THE MURDERER. THE PRODUCERS DID AS HE WISHED AND PLACED HIS NAME FIRST AMONG THE CREDITS AT THE END OF THE MOVIE.

APPROXIMATELY 100 PEOPLE DIE EACH YEAR CHOKING ON BALLPOINT PENS.

AMERICAN DENTISTS RECOMMEND THAT YOU KEEP YOUR TOOTHBRUSH AT LEAST 6 FEET FROM A FLUSHING TOILET. THIS WILL HELP PREVENT UNINVITED AIRBOURNE PARTICLES FROM ALIGHTING ONTO YOUR TOOTHBRUSH AND ENDING UP IN YOUR MOUTH.

THE ABBREVIATION "DVD" STANDS FOR "DIGITAL VERSATILE DISC".

THE SHORTEST MOVIE CRITIQUE IS LEONARD MALTIN'S 1948 REVIEW OF THE FILM *ISN'T IT ROMANTIC?* HIS REVIEW SIMPLY SAID, "NO".

ANOTHER MORE COMPLICATED WORD FOR SQUINTING IS "STRABISMUS".

IN *TOY STORY 2*, A CALENDAR FROM A BUGS LIFE IS BRIEFLY DISPLAYED. BOTH COMPUTER ANIMATED FILMS WERE PRODUCED BY PIXAR.

IN GREEK MYTHOLOGY, EROS IS THE GOD OF LOVE. IN ROMAN MYTHOLOGY, HIS NAME IS AMOR.

WHEN MONTY PYTHON'S FILM *LIFE OF BRIAN* WAS RELEASED IN 1979, IT WAS FORBIDDEN IN NORWAY BUT RELEASED THERE ONE YEAR LATER.

ACCORDING TO LEGEND, AZTEC RULER MONTEZUMA DRANK 50 CUPS OF CHOCOLATE EVERY DAY FROM GOBLETS MADE OF PURE GOLD.

LOS ANGELES FULL NAME IS "EL PUEBLO DE NUESTRA SENORA LA REINA DE LOS ANGELES DE PORCIUNCULA".

HEAVY WATER IS ACTUALLY 10 % HEAVIER THAN ORDINARY WATER.

DANNY DEVITO GOT THE PART OF MARTINI IN THE FILM *ONE FLEW OVER THE CUCKOOS NEST* BECAUSE HE HAD PLAYED THIS SAME ROLE ON BROADWAY A COUPLE OF YEARS EARLIER.

IN 1984, THE BELGIAN ADVENTURER
BRUNO LEUNEN BOUGHT THE
LONGEST TICKET IN THE WORLD FOR
HIS JOURNEY AROUND THE WORLD.
IT INCLUDED 80 AIRLINE COMPANIES
AND 109 INTERMEDIATE
LANDINGS. WHEN THE TICKET WAS
PRINTED OUT, IT WAS 40 FEET LONG!

THE CIGARETTE LIGHTER WAS
INVENTED BEFORE MATCHES WERE.

ALL POLAR BEARS ARE
LEFT HANDED.

WOMEN BLINK ALMOST TWICE AS OFTEN AS MEN DO.

YOU CAN LEAD A COW UPSTAIRS BUT NOT DOWNSTAIRS.

ONLY ONE PERSON IN TWO BILLION WILL LIVE TO BE 116 YEARS OR OLDER.

ELEPHANTS ARE THE ONLY ANIMALS THAT CAN'T JUMP.

YOUR SPINAL MARROW MEASURES
APPROXIMATELY 17 INCHES IN
LENGTH AND ONLY WEIGHS
ABOUT 1 OUNCE.

GENUINE PEARLS MELT WHEN
PUT INTO VINEGAR.

THE TASTEBUDS OF BUTTERFLIES
ARE ON THEIR FEET.

THE LATIN WORD FOR SEALS IS "PINNIPEDIA", WHICH MEANS FIN FOOTED.

IF A TURKEY LOOKS UP WITH ITS MOUTH OPEN WHEN IT'S RAINING, IT COULD DROWN.

THE WORLD'S LONGEST UNIT OF TIME IS THE HINDUS KALPA. IT IS EQUIVALENT TO 4,000,000,032 YEARS, THE TIME IT TAKES TO FLATTEN THE HIMALAYA MOUNTAIN RANGE BY SCRAPING AWAY AT IT WITH A SILK THREAD.

IN EVERY EPISODE OF *SEINFELD*,
YOU CAN SEE SOMETHING WITH
SUPERMAN ON IT.

A MORE THAN 10,000-YEARS-OLD,
A CONIFEROUS TREE, ON THE ISLAND
OF TASMANIA, IS THE OLDEST
KNOWN LIVING ORGANISM. IT HAS
LIVED THROUGH THE CULTURAL
DEVELOPMENT OF MANKIND AND
MAGESTICALLY COVERS AN AREA AS
LARGE AS A CITY BLOCK.

IN THE FILM *GOLD RUSH*, A STARVING CHARLIE CHAPLIN EATS HIS OWN SHOES. THESE SHOES WERE ACTUALLY MADE FROM LIQUORICE.

ONE OF CHINA'S GOALS IS THAT EVERY CITIZEN SHOULD BE ABLE TO EAT 200 EGGS YEARLY. IT IS ESTIMATED THAT IN ORDER TO FEED 1.3 BILLION PEOPLE 200 EGGS A YEAR, THEY REQUIRE 1.3 BILLION HENS WHO MUST EAT MORE GRAIN THAN AUSTRALIA PRODUCES YEARLY.

CERTAIN TROPICAL FISH ARE ABLE
TO CLIMB TREES – SOME UP TO A
HEIGHT OF 32 FEET. MANY OF THEM
ARE SO APT AT BREATHING THEY
WOULD DROWN IF FORCED TO STAY
UNDERWATER FOR TOO LONG.

IN THE STATE OF ARIZONA, IT IS
FORBIDDEN TO LICK A BUFO
ALVARIUS. THIS TOAD SECRETES A
POTENT SUBSTANCE THAT SCARES
PREDATORS AWAY. IT ALSO WORKS
AS A HALLUCINOGENIC DRUG AND
SOME ABUSERS LICK IT OFF THE
TOADS WHILE OTHERS SCRAPE IT
OFF THE SKIN AND SMOKE IT.

BOTTLED WATER COST ALMOST 1,000 TIMES MORE THAN TAP WATER.

ACCORDING TO MATHEMATICAL EXPERTS, A DECK OF CARDS MUST BE SHUFFLED AT LEAST SEVEN TIMES TO AVOID HAVING THEM END UP AS THEY WERE FROM THE START OF THE SHUFFLE.

WHAT DO AMERICANS GET STUCK IN THEIR THROATS MORE THAN ANY OTHER OBJECT? TOOTH PICKS.

IN QUENTIN TARANTINO'S FILM *PULP FICTION*, ALL THE WATCHES SHOW TWENTY MINUTES PAST FOUR O'CLOCK. IT IS SUGGESTED THAT THIS IS A REFERENCE TO THE INVENTOR OF LSD, ALBERT HOFFMAN, WHO TOOK HIS FIRST LSD TRIP ON APRIL 19, 1943 AT 4:20 PM.

ON AVERAGE, A PERSON HAS ABOUT 100,000 HAIRS GROWING ON TOP OF THEIR HEAD AND THEY LOSE BETWEEN 50 TO 100 OF THEM EVERYDAY. A BLOND SPROUTS ABOUT 140,000, A REDHEAD HAS AROUND 90,000 AND A BROWN HAIRED INDIVIDUAL'S HEAD BARES SOMETHING IN BETWEEN.

THERE IS AN INTERNATIONAL SOCIETY WHOSE SOLE PURPOSE IS TO INFORM THE WORLD THAT ALL SCIENTIFIC FACTS ARE FALSE. AMONG OTHER THINGS, ITS MEMBERS MAINTAIN THAT THE EARTH IS FLAT AND THAT THE DISTANCE BETWEEN THE EARTH AND SUN IS 3,221 MILES - NOT 92 MILLION MILES.

BRITAIN'S QUEEN ELIZABETH THE FIRST WAS EXTREMELY GENEROUS WITH HER MAKEUP. WHEN SHE PASSED AWAY, SHE WAS MADE UP WITH A LAYER OF LIPSTICK 1/3 OF AN INCH IN THICKNESS.

WHENEVER YOU SEE A DOG PAWING AT THE GROUND AFTER FINISHING ITS BUSINESS, DO YOU THINK IT'S NEATLY COVERING UP ITS POO? WELL, IT'S NOT. THEY ARE LEAVING TRACES OF THEIR UNIQUE SCENT BEHIND, WHICH IS RELEASED FROM ODOUR GLANDS ON THE BOTTOM OF THEIR PAWS.

WHEN FLYING DOMESTIC WITHIN THE USA, STATISTICALLY YOU MUST FLY EVERYDAY FOR 19,000 YEARS BEFORE HAVING AN ACCIDENT.

IT'S MORE STRAINING FOR THE VOCAL CHORDS TO WHISPER THAN TO SPEAK IN A NORMAL VOICE.

THE TRANS-SIBERIAN RAILWAY IS A 5,778-MILE LONG ROUTE THROUGH RUSSIA, FROM MOSCOW TO VLADIVOSTOK. EARLIER TRAVELLERS HAD TO TAKE THIS JOURNEY BY BOAT ACROSS LAKE BAIKAL. A ONE WAY TRIP ON THE TRANS-SIBERIAN RAILWAY TAKES 7 LONG DAYS.

IN 1964, THE FIRST LASER WAS REPRODUCED ON FILM IN *GOLDFINGER.*

IN 1969, APOLLO 1 TOOK THE FIRST
MAN TO THE MOON.
ITS STEERING SYSTEM WAS LESS
ADVANCED THAN COMPUTERS AND
CALCULATORS ARE TODAY.

DAVID PROWSE DID NOT KNOW THAT
FELLOW ACTOR JAMES EARL JONES
WAS GIVING HIS VOICE TO PROWSE'S
CHARACTER, DARTH VADER, IN THE
MOVIE *STAR WARS*.
HE FIRST NOTICED WHILE WATCHING
THE PREMIERE.

SWEDEN'S GLOBEN ARENA, BUILT IN STOCKHOLM BETWEEN 1986 AND 1988, IS THE LARGEST SPHERICAL BUILDING IN THE WORLD.

A RECENTLY DISCOVERED SPECIES OF ANTS HAS BEEN NAMED AFTER HARRISON FORD. THE SPECIES IS CALLED PEIDOLE HARRISONFORDI.

IF YOU DON'T COVER YOUR MOUTH WHILE SNEEZING, 20,000 SMALL DROPLETS OF SALIVA CAN FORCEFULLY PROJECT FROM YOUR MOUTH UP TO 13-FEET AWAY.

YOU WILL NEVER FIND SEEDS IN
CLEMENTINES BUT YOU WILL FIND
THEM IN MANDARINES,
THE ORIGINAL FRUIT. THE SEED FREE
VARIETY WAS NAMED AFTER HIS
CREATOR, THE FRENCH PRIEST
CLEMENT, WHO AROUND 1900,
DEVELOPED IT.

THE THIGHBONE AND SHINBONE
CAN BE EXPOSED TO A VERTICAL
PRESSURE UP TO 2,200 POUNDS,
WITHOUT BREAKING
- THE WEIGHT OF AN AVERAGE CAR.

DURING AN AVERAGE LIFETIME OF
70 YEARS YOU WILL BREATH 600
MILLION TIMES, FEEL 125 MILLION
HEART BEATS, AND YOUR EYES WILL
BLINK 350 MILLION TIMES.

THE DAILY PRODUCTION OF GASES
IN YOUR LARGE INTESTINE
MEASURES 2 TO 2.5 GALLONS.
YOU WILL EMIT ABOUT 0.2 GALLONS
OF THIS WHILE YOUR INTESTINAL
WALL ABSORBS THE REST.

THE GUINNESS BOOK OF RECORDS CLAIMS THAT "MY NAME IS BOND, JAMES BOND" IS THE MOST FAMOUS MOVIE LINE IN THE WORLD.

THE GERMANS UNMASKED SEVERAL AMERICAN SPIES DURING THE SECOND WORLD WAR BY STUDYING HOW THEY ATE. THE AMERICANS CUT THEIR STEAKS IN SMALLER PIECES BEFORE THEY ATE IT.

THE LARGEST KIDNEY STONE IN THE HISTORY OF MEDICINE WEIGHED 14 POUNDS.

THE SMALLEST BIRD IN THE WORLD IS THE 2.3-INCH HUMMINGBIRD. IT COUNTERACTS THE FORCES OF GRAVITY BY FLAPPING ITS WINGS OVER 200 TIMES PER SECOND.

BETWEEN THE YEARS OF 1788 AND 1868, GREAT BRITAIN DEPORTED 155,000 PRISONERS TO THEIR COLONY AUSTRALIA.

IF THE EARTH WAS ABSOLUTELY SMOOTH AND FLAT, IT WOULD BE COVERED WITH A LAYER OF WATER 500-FEET DEEP.

IN THE POPULAR BOND FILM *FROM RUSSIA WITH LOVE*, AUTHOR IAN FLEMMING MADE A CAMEO APPEARANCE IN ONE OF THE SCENE AS A MAN TAKING A LEISURELY WALK.

RUBBER BANDS LAST LONGER IF KEPT COLD.

THE FIRST DEPORTATION TO SIBERIA IN RUSSIA WAS NOT A HUMAN BUT A SYMBOL – THE CITY BELL OF UGLICH. IN 1591, THE SON OF THE TSAR WAS MURDERED AND ANGRY CITIZENS RANG THE QUARTER TON BELL IN PROTEST. AS PUNISHMENT AND A DEMONSTRATION OF POWER, THESE AGITATORS WERE BEATEN AND THEIR TONGUES WERE CUT OFF. THE BELL WAS ALSO HAMMERED AND IT CLAPPER WAS PULLED AWAY FROM ITS HOLD. AS A FINAL DISPLAY, THE BELL WAS DEPORTED TO SIBERIA TO BE SILENCED FOREVER.

IDLING BOAT ENGINES HAVE
ACOUSTICAL CHARACTERISTICS
REMINISCENT OF GREY WHALES
SINGING. IN MEXICO, FISHERMAN
HAVE PROBLEMS WITH WHALES
RUBBING THEIR BACKS AGAINST
THEIR FISHING VESSELS.

DON'T TRY THIS – IF YOU TAKE A
VERY SHARP PENCIL, DIP THE VERY
TIP IN NICOTINE AND PUSH THIS
THROUGH YOUR SKIN,
YOU WILL DIE IMMEDIATELY.

JUST BEFORE YOU FREEZE TO DEATH, YOUR BODY'S SENSE OF TEMPERATURE BREAKS DOWN AND MAKES A PERSON FEEL LIKE HE OR SHE IS ON FIRE. THIS IS WHY SOME PEOPLE, FOUND DEAD IN THE WINTERTIME, ARE UNDRESSED.

SOME OCTOPUSES LIVE IN SUCH DEEP WATER, IT IS COMPLETELY DARK ALL THE TIME. HERE IT IS USELESS FOR THEM TO SQUIRT BLACK INK AT THEIR ENEMIES TO CONFUSE THEM. INSTEAD, THE OCTOPUSES EMIT A CLOUD OF LUMINOUS GERMS THAT BLIND THEIR PREDATORS.

MARILYN MONROE HAD SIX TOES ON HER LEFT FOOT.

THE WHITE HALF SHAPED MOON ON YOUR FINGERS IS A SMALL, AIR FILLED POCKET. NO ONE KNOWS WHY IT'S THERE.

IF YOU TOOK ALL THE WHEAT THAT IS CONSUMED AROUND THE WORLD DURING A YEAR AND BAKED A LOAF OF BREAD FROM IT, THAT LOAF WOULD BE ABOUT 13-FEET IN DIAMETER, 6.5-FEET HIGH AND LONG ENOUGH TO GO AROUND THE EARTH ONCE.

ONCE UPON A TIME, DISNEY'S CARTOON CHARACTER, DONALD DUCK, WAS BANNED IN FINLAND BECAUSE HE DIDN'T WEAR PANTS.

LEGO WAS INVENTED IN 1949. THE NAME COMES FROM THE DANISH WORDS "LEG", MEANING PLAY AND "GODT" MEANING GOOD.

THE STATE OF NEW JERSEY, USA PROVIDES TWO THIRDS OF THE WORLD'S TOTAL PRODUCTION OF EGGPLANT.

THE PHILOSOPHER, RENÉ DESCARTES, WHO CONSIDERED HIMSELF TO BE THE INVENTOR OF THE FIRST PHILOSOPHI-CAL PRINCIPLE – COGITO ERGO SUM (I THINK, THEREFORE, I AM), - DIED WHILE VISITING QUEEN KRISTINA IN 1649. THE CASTLE WAS VERY COLD AND DESCARTES SUFFERED FROM PNEUMONIA, WHICH KILLED HIM.

THERE ARE MORE CHICKENS THAN HUMANS ON OUR PLANET.

THE SPANISH FLY IS THE WORLD'S MOST FAMOUS BUG. SOME BELIEVE IT HAS APHRODISIAC PROPERTIES. ONE THING IS FOR CERTAIN. DRIED AND POWDERED, SPANISH FLIES MAKE A POTENT POISON AND MANY HAVE DIED FROM IT. THE LAST KNOWN CASE WAS IN THE 1960'S.

AL CAPONE'S BUSINESS CARD SAID THAT HE WAS A USED FURNITURE SALESMAN.

A GOLDFISH CAN ONLY REMEMBER THE LAST THREE SECONDS OF ITS LIFE.

MORE SHOPLIFTERS ARE CAUGHT ON A WEDNESDAY THAN ANY OTHER DAY OF THE WEEK.

WE ARE BORN WITHOUT KNEECAPS. THEY DEVELOP AT THE AGE OF SIX.

WILLIAM SHAKESPEARE "INVENTED" MORE THAN 1,700 WORDS.

THE WORLD FAMOUS OPERA HOUSE IN SYDNEY, AUSTRALIA WAS DESIGNED BY THE DANISH ARCHITECT JÖRN UTZON. IT´S COVERED WITH OVER ONE MILLION WHITE CERAMIC BOARDS, MANUFACTURED BY THE SWEDISH COMPANY HÖGANÄS.

DO YOU WANT TO BUY A CAMEL? THE LARGEST EXPORTER OF CAMELS IN THE WESTERN WORLD IS NORWAY.

YOUR EYES REMAIN THE SAME IN SIZE FROM THE DAY YOU ARE BORN TO THE DAY YOU DIE. YOUR NOSE AND EARS, HOWEVER, WILL NEVER STOP GROWING.

THE TAME CAT CAME TO SCANDINAVIA ABOUT 1,500 YEARS AGO. BEFORE THAT ONE OFTEN HAD – A TAME SNAKE!

EVERY YEAR, MORE PEOPLE GET KILLED BY DONKEYS THAN PLANE CRASHES.

YOU NEED 150,000 SAFFRON
CROCUSES TO GET TWO POUNDS
OF SAFFRON.

THE SPERM WHALE HAS THE LARGEST
BRAIN OF ALL ANIMALS IN THE
WORLD. IT WEIGHS 20 POUNDS.

FROGS NEVER DRINK WATER.
THEY GET ALL THE FLUID THEY
NEED BY LIVING IN A WET
AND MOIST ENVIRONMENT.

THE LARGEST CONCENTRATION OF ANIMALS EVER OBSERVED WAS A HUGE SWARM OF GRASSHOPPERS IN 1879. THE SWARM WAS THE SIZE OF GERMANY AND CONTAINED MORE THAN 12,500 BILLION INSECTS THAT TOGETHER WEIGHED ABOUT 55,000 BILLION POUNDS.

IN RELATION TO THEIR SIZE, BUGS THAT BELONG TO THE SPECIES SCARABEIDAE ARE THE STRONGEST ANIMALS IN THE WORLD. WHEN TESTS WERE DONE ON THE QUITE RARE ORYCTES NASICORNIS, IT WAS FOUND THAT IT COULD CARRY 850 TIMES ITS OWN WEIGHT ON ITS BACK.

A STRANGE FASHION COLOUR WAS CREATED BY THE SOVEREIGN QUEEN ISABELLA, THE DAUGHTER OF FILIP II OF SPAIN. IN 1601, SHE SWORE NOT TO CHANGE HER UNDERWEAR UNTIL THE CITY OF OOSTENDE WAS TAKEN. UNFORTUNATELY, THE OCCUPATION LASTED FOR THREE YEARS SO ISABELLA'S UNDERWEAR GOT THE BEIGE COLOUR THAT TODAY IS KNOWN AS ISABELLA COLOURED.

DENTAL ENAMEL IS THE STRONGEST MATERIAL YOUR BODY CAN PRODUCE.

WHEN CHARLIE CHAPLIN BECAME FAMOUS FOR HIS MOVIES, A LOT OF PEOPLE STARTED TO DRESS AND ACT LIKE HIM. EVEN CHARLIE CHAPLIN LOOK-A-LIKE CONTESTS WERE HELD. CHARLIE PARTICIPATED IN ONE HIMSELF – AND WON THIRD PLACE.

A STARFISH HAS VERY BAD TABLE MANNERS. IT TURNS ITS STOMACH INSIDE OUT, BY FORCING IT OUT THROUGH ITS MOUTH AND OVER ITS PREY.

THE "BLACK BOX" EVERYONE IS
LOOKING FOR AFTER A PLANE CRASH
IS NOT BLACK – IT´S ORANGE,
MAKING IT EASIER TO FIND. BESIDES,
THERE´S NOT ONLY ONE BOX, BUT
TWO. ONE IS USED FOR RECORDING
ALL CONVERSATIONS AND SOUNDS IN
THE COCKPIT AND THE OTHER TO
SAVE ALL DATA FROM THE FLIGHT.

WHEN YOU TAKE A NAP FOR AN
HOUR YOU BURN AS MUCH ENERGY
AS IT TAKES TO BOIL WATER FOR
SEVEN CUPS OF TEA.

THE SHORTEST WAR IN WORLD
HISTORY WAS FOUGHT BETWEEN
GREAT BRITAIN AND ZANZIBAR,
THE 27TH OF AUGUST, 1896.
IT LASTED ONLY 38 MINUTES.

IF YOUR HEART MUSCLE WAS
REQUIRED TO WORK FILLING BEER
BOTTLES IN A BREWERY, IT WOULD
BE ABLE TO FILL DAILY 1,600 CRATES
OF BEER WITH 30 BOTTLES EACH AND
IT WOULD WORK, WITHOUT REQUIR-
ING ANY REPAIRS, FOR 70 YEARS.

IF YOU MULTIPLY THE NUMBER OF
INHABITANTS IN THE USA BY 2,
YOU'LL GET THE NUMBER OF CREDIT
CARDS USED IN THAT COUNTRY.

ADOLF HITLER HAD
ONLY ONE TESTICLE.

A FIVE MONTHS OLD FOETUS HAS
MORE HAIR ON ITS BACK THAN
AN ADULT GORILLA.

NOT SO LONG AGO, WHEN A PRISONER ESCAPED FROM THE ALAMOS PRISON IN MEXICO, THE RESPONSIBLE GUARD WAS SENTENCED TO SERVING THE REMAINING TIME ON THE PRISONER'S SENTENCE.

AIR FORCE PILOTS HAVE MORE DAUGHTERS (DETERMINED BY THE X-CHROMOSOME) THAN SONS (DETERMINED BY THE Y-CHROMOSOME) BECAUSE THE X-CHROMOSOME TOLERATES THE MORE STRESSFUL EFFECTS OF GRAVITY BETTER THAN THE Y-CHROMOSOME DOES.

ON AVERAGE, A HUMAN BEING HAS EIGHTEEN BLEMISHES ON HIS OR HER BODY.

A VULTURE'S STOMACH IS SO ACIDIC THAT JUST AFTER A COUPLE OF HOURS IT CAN DISSOLVE A NAIL.

FOR EACH HUMAN BEING ON EARTH, THERE ARE MORE THAN HALF A MILLION INSECTS.

ONE SINGLE TREE CAN BE HOME TO 20 MILLION LICE.

SPERM ARE CREATED IN THE MALE TESTICLES. THE TESTICLES ARE CONSTRUCTED SO THEY BUILD PIPE-FORMED STRUCTURES, AND IN EVERY TESTICLE THESE PIPES ARE MORE THAN 400 YARDS LONG.

A SINGLE THREAD IN A SPIDER'S WEB IS AS STRONG AS A STEEL CABLE OF THE SAME SIZE.

THE DIVISION OF BLOOD GROUPS VARIES BETWEEN DIFFERENT PEOPLE IN DIFFERENT COUNTRIES. THE ONLY GROUP OF PEOPLE WHO HAVE THE SAME BLOOD GROUP ARE AMERICAN NATIVES – O.

IN INDIA, WHERE HINDUISM IS THE MAJOR RELIGION, THEY WORSHIP OVER 300 MILLION GODS. ALMOST EVERY LITTLE VILLAGE HAS ITS OWN LOCAL GOD.

EVERY SINGLE SECOND, YOUR MARROW PRODUCES ABOUT 3 MILLION RED BLOOD CORPUSCLES. DURING THAT TIME, THE SAME AMOUNT DIE. THE DAILY PRODUCTION IS MORE THAN 200 BILLION CORPSUCLES.

ON AVERAGE, THERE ARE 94 GIRLS BORN FOR EVERY 100 BOYS, BUT AMONG QUADRUPLETS, 156 GIRLS ARE BORN FOR EVERY 100 BOYS.

IT HAS BEEN PROVEN THAT TALLER PEOPLE PRESENT BETTER RESULTS ON INTELLIGENCE TESTS.

ABOUT 1,000 DOWN FEATHERS CAN BE PRESSED INTO A THIMBLE. ONCE REMOVED, THEY WILL SOON REGAIN THEIR ORIGINAL VOLUME.

THE FIRST NOSE TRANSPLANTS WERE PERFORMED IN INDIA AS EARLY AS 750 B.C. THE NOSES WERE TAKEN FROM UNFAITHFUL WIVES.

THE ACIDITY IN THE HUMAN STOMACH IS SO STRONG THAT IT HAS TO BE DILUTED ABOUT 400 TIMES TO REACH THE SAME GRADE OF SOURNESS AS COCA COLA.

RADIUM 224 IS THE MOST POISONOUS ELEMENT IN THE WORLD. THIS ISOTOPE IS NATURALLY COMMON AND 17,000 TIMES MORE POISONOUS THAN PLUTONIUM 239.

WHEN IAN FLEMING WROTE HIS FIRST BOOK *CASINO ROYALE*, HE GOT THE NAME JAMES BOND FROM A WRITER OF A BOOK ABOUT CARIBBEAN BIRDS.

MEL BLANC, THE MAN WHO GAVE VOICE TO *BUGS BUNNY*, WAS ALLERGIC TO CARROTS.

BULLETPROOF VESTS, FIRE LADDERS, WINDSHIELD WIPERS, AND LASER PRINTERS WERE ALL INVENTED BY WOMEN.

THE THREE WISE MEN WERE NAMED
CASPAR, MELCHIOR AND BALTHAZAR.

THIEVES OFTEN LISTEN AT DOORS
AND IN SOME CASES THIS HAS
GOTTEN THEM CONVICTED. THE
POLICE ARE NOT ONLY INTERESTED IN
FINGERPRINTS BUT EAR PRINTS AS
WELL, WHICH ARE UNIQUE FOR EVERY
HUMAN BEING.

IN INDIA, MORE THAN 140 MAIN
LANGUAGES ARE SPOKEN WITH
845 ACCENTS.

NEW SPECIES CAN BE FOUND IN
THE STRANGEST PLACES. A NEW ANT
SPECIES WAS FOUND IN A FLOWER
POT ON THE SIXTEENTH FLOOR OF
A GERMAN OFFICE BUILDING.

51,000 PEOPLE CAN FIT ONTO A
FOOTBALL FIELD IF THEY STAND
REALLY CLOSE TOGETHER.

IF YOU ARE AFRAID OF
ANIMALS IN GENERAL, YOU
SUFFER FROM ZOOPHOBIA.

THE CAPE OF GOOD HOPE IS NOT THE MOST SOUTHERN PART OF AFRICA. IT IS CAP AGULHA, WHICH IS LOCATED ABOUT 90 MILES SOUTH-EAST OF THE CAPE OF GOOD HOPE.

ON AVERAGE EVERY YEAR, YOU WILL CONSUME 12 PUBIC HAIRS WHILE EATEN IN RESTAURANTS.

THE NATIONAL ANTHEM OF THE EUROPEAN UNION (EU) IS *AN DER FREUDE FROM THE NINTH SYMPHONY* BY LUDVIG VON BEETHOVEN.

JOHN WILKES BOOTH, THE MAN WHO
SHOT ABRAHAM LINCOLN, THE 16TH
PRESIDENT OF THE USA,
WAS AN ACTOR.

ONE OF THE ELEMENTS IN
DYNAMITE IS PEANUTS.

THE FIVE DIFFERENT COLOURED
RINGS, ON THE OLYMPIC FLAG,
SYMBOLIZES THE UNION OF THE FIVE
CONTINENTS AND THAT THE OLYMIC
GAMES SHALL BE A MEETING PLACE
FOR ATHLETES FROM AROUND THE
WORLD. AT LEAST ONE COLOUR OF
THE RINGS CAN BE FOUND IN EVERY
WORLD FLAG.

SEAN CONNERY, THE FIRST JAMES
BOND, WON THE MR. UNIVERSE CON-
TEST BEFORE HE BECAME AN ACTOR.

A CAT HAS THIRTY-TWO
MUSCLES IN EACH EAR.

DID YOU THINK THAT THE MONKEYS
IN THE ZOO WERE PICKING FLEAS OFF
EACH OTHER?
WRONG; THEY ARE IN FACT
GROOMING FOR SALTY SKIN DANDER.

WHEN YOU'RE USING THE
COMPUTER KEYBOARD,
YOUR LEFT HAND DOES
56% OF THE TYPING.

THE ACTUAL MEANING OF THE WORD
TURKEY IS "COCK FROM CALICUT".

THE ZIPPER WOULD NOT HAVE
BECOME THE SUCCESS IT DID IF IT
HADN'T BEEN FOR WORLD WAR ONE.
ORIGINALLY, IT WASN'T USED ON
CLOTHING BUT ON MONEY BELTS
THAT THE AMERCIAN SOLDERS
BROUGHT TO EUROPE.

**MANY HAMSTERS BLINK
ONLY ONE EYE AT A TIME.**

**THE PACEMAKER WAS INVENTED IN
THE 1950'S BY SWEDEN'S RUNE
ELMQVIST AT THE PACESETTER
COMPANY.**

**THE CHANCE OF SURVIVING A FLIGHT
ACCIDENT IS BETTER IN THE BACK
SEATS OF A PLANE WHERE YOU HAVE
THE BEST PROTECTION DURING TAKE
OFFS AND LANDINGS. THIS IS WHEN
THE RISK OF AN ACCIDENT IS AT ITS
GREATEST.**

IF BARBIE HAD BEEN A REAL HUMAN BEING, HER MEASUREMENTS WOULD HAVE BEEN 97-58-97.

IT'S OFTEN WARMER IN CITIES THAN IN THE COUNTRYSIDE. THE REASON BEING ASPHALT ABSORBS MORE ENERGY FROM THE SUN THAN GRASS, TREES, AND PLANTS DO.

THE LONGEST BORDER BETWEEN TWO STATES IN EUROPE IS THE BORDER BETWEEN SWEDEN AND NORWAY. IT'S 1,000 MILES LONG.

JOHN RHYS-DAVIES, WHO PLAYED GIMLI THE DWARF IN THE THREE *LORD OF THE RINGS* MOVIES HAD A TOUGH TIME DURING FILMING. HIS ARMAMENT WEIGHED 66 POUNDS AND HE WAS ALSO ALLERGIC TO THE PROSTHETIC GLUE.

AT FIRST, CINDERELLA'S SHOES WERE MADE OF LEATHER BUT WHEN THE FOLKTALE WAS WRITTEN DOWN IN THE 16TH CENTURY, THE FRENCH WORDS "VAIR" AND "VERRE" WERE MIXED UP. THE FIRST MEANS SKIN AND THE LATTER MEANS GLASS.

ON AVERAGE, A HURRICAN PRODUCES MORE ENERGY THAN ALL OF THE WORLD'S POWER PLANTS PUT TOGETHER.

IN 1899, THE EIFFEL TOWER WAS BUILT BY GUSTAVE EIFFEL FOR THE PARIS EXHIBITION AND WAS SUPPOSE TO BE DEMOLISHED AFTERWARDS.

ONE DAY – THE TIME IT TAKES OUR PLANET TO ROTATE AROUND ITSELF – IS ONLY 9 HOURS AND 55 MINUTES ON THE PLANET JUPITER.

THE AFRICAN OSTRICH IS NOT ONLY
THE LARGEST BIRD IN THE WORLD-
IT ALSO LAYS THE LARGEST EGGS.
ON AVERAGE, ONE EGG WEIGHS 2 TO
4 POUNDS.
THAT'S EQUIVALENT TO THE WEIGHT
OF 45 NORMAL-SIZED EGGS.

IF YOU NEVER CUT YOUR HAIR AND
LIVE TO BE 77 YEARS OLD, YOUR
HAIR COULD GROW 690 MILES LONG.

A NEWBORN KANGAROO WEIGHS
APPROXIMATELY ONE GRAM
(0,035 OUNCES).

HURRICANES ARE ALWAYS GIVEN
NAMES IN ORDER TO MAKE THEM
EASIER TO TRACK. THEIR NAMES
ALWAYS START WITH AN "A" AT THE
BEGINNING OF EACH YEAR.
IN 1979, THE WOMEN'S MOVEMENT
PRESSURED METEOROLOGISTS TO
USE BOTH MALE AND FEMALE NAMES
INSTEAD OF JUST FEMALE NAMES.
TODAY, BOY NAMES ARE USED ON
EVEN NUMBERED YEARS AND GIRL
NAMES ON UNEVEN ONES.

VOLVO MEANS
"I AM ROLLING"
IN LATIN.

PRODUCTION SUFFERED A SEVERE CATASTROPHE ONE-DAY WHILE FILMING *DIAMONDS ARE FOREVER*. UNEXPECTEDLY, ALL OF THE TROPICAL FISH IN THE AQUARIUM DIED. THE SOLUTION WAS TO FREEZE THE FISH AND SUSPEND THEM IN THE TANK FROM INVISIBLE THREAD THAT COULD BE MOVED; MAKING THEM APPEAR ALIVE.

IT IS IMPOSSIBLE TO SNEEZE WITH YOUR EYES OPEN.

AN ICE CREAM HEADACHE OCCURS WITH THE COLDNESS OF THE ICE CREAM COMES IN CONTACT WITH A SPIDER-SHAPED WEB OF NERVES ON THE ROOF OF THE MOUTH. WHEN THE TEMPERATURE OF THESE NERVES COOLS DOWN, THE BRAIN BELIEVES THAT IT'S ABOUT TO FREEZE AND UNNECESSARILY SENDS WARM BLOOD TO THE AREA. INSTEAD OF WARMING THE AREA, IT CAUSES A HEADACHE.

THE FACE OF THE ALIEN E.T IN THE FILM WITH THE SAME NAME, WAS MODELLED AFTER THE POET CARL SANDBURG, THE PHYSICIST ALBERT EINSTEIN, AND A PUG.

THE PLANE BUDDY HOLLY CRASHED
IN WAS NAMED "AMERICAN PIE".
DON MCLEAN ADOPTED THIS NAME
FOR A SONG HE RELEASED A COUPLE
OF YEARS LATER.

THE SLOTH MOVES SO SLOW ALGAE
CAN GROW UNHINDERRED ON IT.
THAT IS WHY ITS SKIN IS
SOMETIMES GREEN.

IT´S NOT ONLY THE TIGER'S FUR
THAT IS STRIPED.
THE SKIN IS STRIPED AS WELL.

THE EXPRESSION "CHECKMATE" COMES FROM THE ARABIC EXPRES-SION "SHAH MAT", WHICH MEANS "THE KING IS DEAD".

DO YOU THINK "BIG BEN" IS A TOWER OR A CLOCK FACE? WELL, BOTH ARE GUESSES WRONG. THIS WELL-KNOWN NAME ACTUALLY BELONGS TO THE BELL THAT SOUNDS EVERY HOUR BEHIND THE FAMOUS CLOCK FACE IN LONDON, ENGLAND.

WHEN THE NORTH AMERICAN POSSUM IS THREATENED, IT NOT ONLY PLAYS DEAD TO ESCAPE THE DANGER.
IT ALSO FAINTS FROM FEAR!

SESAME STREET PUPPET CHARAC-
TERS BERTAND ERNIE'S NAMESAKES
ARE THE POLICEMAN, BERT AND TAXI
DRIVER, ERNIE, APPEARING IN THE
CLASSIC FILM *IT'S A WONDERFUL
LIFE* STARRING JIMMY STEWART.

DID YOU KNOW THAT CAMELS HAVE
THREE EYELASHES TO PROTECT THEIR
EYES FROM THE BLOWING SAND?

A DONKEY'S EYES ARE POSITIONED
SO THAT IT CAN SEE ALL OF ITS
HOOVES AT THE SAME TIME.

WHEN YOU'RE BORN, YOU HAVE 300 BONES IN YOUR BODY BUT WHEN YOU DIE, YOU ONLY HAVE 206.

THE ONLY KNOWN MONTH TO NOT HAVE A FULL MOON IS FEBRUARY 1865.

ACCORDING TO THE AUTHOR IAN FLEMING, JAMES BOND'S FATHER WAS FROM SCOTLAND AND HIS MOTHER FROM FRANCE.

AN OSTRICH'S EYE IS LARGER THAN ITS BRAIN.

THE TOASTER WAS INTRODUCED BY GENERAL ELECTRIC IN THE USA IN 1909.

THE LEANING TOWER OF PISA, ONE OF ITALY'S GREATEST TOURIST ATTRACTIONS, LEANS IN A SOUTHERLY DIRECTION.

THE LATIN INSCRIPTION I.N.R.I.
STAND FOR "IESUS NAZARENUS, REX
IUDAEORUM" WHICH MEANS "JESUS
OF NAZARETH, KING OF THE JEWS".

DURING THE SECOND WORLD WAR,
QUEEN ELIZABETH II STUDIED TO
BECOME A CAR MECHANIC.

IN PARAGUAY, DUELLING IS ONLY
LEGAL IF BOTH FIGHTERS ARE
REGISTERED BLOOD DONORS.

A DIAMOND'S WEIGHT IS MEASURED IN CARATS. ORIGINALLY, ONE CARAT EQUALLED THE WEIGHT OF ONE SEED FROM A LOAF OF ST. JOHN'S BREAD. IT WAS CHANGED IN 1931 THAT THE EXACT WEIGHT WAS TO BE 0.2 GRAMS.

SOUTH AFRICA HAS ELEVEN MAIN LANGUAGES, WHICH EXPLAINS WHY, YOU CAN SOMETIMES FIND REALLY LONG ROAD SIGNS. EVERYONE MUST BE ABLE TO READ THEM!

THE EARTH WEIGHS ABOUT 5,924,000,000,000,000,000,000 METRIC TONS.

CONTRARY TO POPULAR BELIEF, THOMAS ALVA EDISON DID NOT INVENT THE LIGHTBULB. MANY HAD DONE THIS BEFORE HIM. WHAT HE DID, HOWEVER, WAS MODIFY THE LIGHTBULB AND PATENT IT.

AN ANGRY MALE HUMMINGBIRD HAS A PULSE UP TO 1,000 BEATS PER MINUTE WHILE, AT THE SAME TIME, DRAWING ABOUT 500 BREATHS.

IN 1820, SCIENTISTS BELIEVED THE UNIVERSE TO BE 6,000 YEARS OLD. TODAY, EXPERTS DATE IT BETWEEN 15 TO 20 BILLION YEARS OLD.

A BLACK HOLE IS A COLLAPSED STAR THAT HAS TURNED INTO A TINY BLACK GLOBE. THE HOLE IS BLACK BECAUSE OF ITS ENORMOUS FORCE OF GRAVITY THAT WON'T LET ANY LIGHT OUT.

SOME MALE SPIDERS HAVE VERY INTERESTING SURVIVAL TECHNIQUES. TO AVOID BEING EATEN BY A FEMALE, THE MALE SPIDER WILL ENTWINE HER IN A COBWEB BEFORE MATING.

IN LONDON, ENGLAND'S FIRE OF 1666, HALF OF THE CITY BURNT DOWN, BUT MIRACULOUSLY ONLY SIX PEOPLE WAS INJURED.

THE OSCAR STATUES ARE NORMALLY MADE OF TIN AND COPPER, BUT DURING THE SECOND WORLD WAR, THEY WERE MADE OF PLASTER, COVERED IN GOLD. ALL METAL WAS NEEDED FOR THE WAR EFFORT.

MOSQUITOES LIVE ON NECTAR NOT BLOOD. BLOOD IS REQUIRED FOR PRODUCING PROTEIN WHICH IS NECESSARY FOR LAYING EGGS.

IF ALL SALT COULD BE EXTRACTED FROM THE SEA AND OCEANS, IT COULD COMPLETELY COVER THE CONTINENTS WITH A 20-INCH LAYER.

THE MOTTO ON JAMES BOND'S
FAMILY WEAPON SHIELD IS
"THE WORLD IS NOT ENOUGH".

PURE GOLD IS SO SOFT THAT YOU
CAN SHAPE IT WITH YOUR HANDS.

ONE HORSEPOWER IS THE FORCE
NEEDED TO LIFT 75 KILOS ONE METER
STRAIGHT UP IN THE AIR
FOR ONE SECOND.

26 POPES HAVE UNFORTUNATELY BEEN MURDERED.

FOR A LONG TIME, THE TONGA ISLANDS HAD A BANANA SHAPED STAMP.

IF YOU SUFFER FROM ARACHINOPHOBIA, YOU´RE TERRIFIED OF SPIDERS.

GEOGRAPHICAL LOCATIONS WITH THE SHORTEST NAMES ARE "A" IN NORWAY, "O" IN JAPAN AND "Y" IN FRANCE.

IF YOU KEEP A LIVING GOLDFISH IN AN COMPLETELY DARK ROOM, IT WILL EVENTUALLY TURN WHITE.

THE HORSEHEAD, USED IN THE FILM *THE GODFATHER*, CAME FROM A FACTORY THAT MANUFACTURES DOG FOOD.

THE A-SYSTEM USED TO KEEP
CONTROL OF PAPER SIZES (A4, A5,
A3 ETC) WAS INVENTED IN GERMANY
IN 1930 AND BECAME
AN INTERNATIONAL STANDARD.

THERE ARE OVER 500 PHOBIAS AND
TAURAPHOBIA IS ONE OF THEM –
A FEAR OF BULLS.

ICE CREAM CONTAINS A THICKENING-
SUBSTANCE EXTRACTED FROM
SEAWEED.

SINCE 1989, OSCAR PRESENTERS ARE NOT ALLOWED TO SAY "AND THE WINNER IS..." THIS INSINUATES THAT ALL OF THE OTHER NOMINEES ARE LOSERS. SO INSTEAD THEY SAY "AND THE OSCAR GOES TO..."

BIRD'S FEET ARE ALWAYS COLD.

THE KOALA BEAR GOT ITS NAME FROM THE AUSTRALIAN ABORIGINALS. KOALA MEANS "NO DRINK" AND REFERS TO THE FACT THAT KOALA BEARS GET ALL THE FLUID THEY NEED EATING EUCALYPTUS LEAVES.

ONE OF THE FIRST MOBILE PHONES WITH A BATTERY SMALLER THAN A BAG WAS THE NMT900 PHONE CURT, FROM ERICSSON. IT WEIGHED 1.6 POUNDS AND YOU COULD TALK ON IT FOR 12 MINUTES.

NICHOLAS CAGE CHANGED HIS LAST NAME FROM COPPOLA TO CAGE SO THAT NO ONE WOULD KNOW THAT HE WAS RELATED TO OSCAR-WINNING DIRECTOR FRANCIS FORD COPPOLA, WHO IS HIS UNCLE.

LEPROSY CAN AFFECT ALL PEOPLE BUT ONLY ONE ANIMAL - THE SOUTH AND MIDDLE AMERICAN ARMADILLO.

EVERY YEAR, THE MOON MOVES 1.5 INCHES AWAY FROM THE EARTH.

BRONTOPHOBIA MEANS A TERRIBLE FEAR OF LIGHTNING.

DIAMONDS ARE MADE OF CARBON AND CAN BURN. IF HEATED UP TO 800°C (1,600°F), DIAMONDS TURN INTO GRAPHITE.

IN THE FAMOUS FILM *CASABLANCA*,
RICK (PLAYED BY HUMPHREY
BOGART) NEVER ONCE SAID,
"PLAY IT AGAIN SAM".
HE ACTUALLY SAID, "YOU PLAYED IT
FOR HER. YOU CAN PLAY IT FOR ME.
PLAY IT!" THE LINE "PLAY IT AGAIN
SAM" ACTUALLY COMES FROM THE
MARX BROTHER'S FILM *ONE NIGHT
IN CASABLANCA*.

A LEECH CAN SUCK UP AS MUCH AS
2 CUBIC CENTIMETERS (0,12 CUBIC
INCHES) OF BLOOD, BUT ONLY AFTER
FASTING FOR A YEAR.

THE FASTEST ANIMAL IN THE WORLD
IS A SWIFT, THAT CAN REACH UP TO
98 MILES PER HOUR (168 KM/H).

THE GIVEN NAME "WENDY" FIRST
APPEARED IN THE BOOK *PETER PAN*.

AN OLYMPIC SPORT IN 1906 WAS
SHOT-PUTTING USING STONES.

BEFORE RONALD REAGAN BECAME
A MOVIE STAR, HE WAS A SPORTS
COMMENTATOR.

LEONARDO DICAPRIOS' FIRST
APPEARANCE IN FRONT OF A CAMERA
WAS IN A COMMERCIAL FOR MILK.

THE HEART OF AN EMBRYO STARTS
BEATING THREE WEEKS FROM
CONCEPTION.

A BLUE WHALE'S PENIS IS BETWEEN
15 – 20 FEET LONG.

THE MOST COMMON DISEASE TO
PLAGUE HUMANS IS "CORYZA",
BETTER KNOWN AS "THE COMMON
COLD". IT HAS SPREAD ALMOST
EVERYWHERE ON EARTH.

THE SMALLEST COUNTRY IN THE
WORLD IS THE VATICAN IN ROME.
IT'S ONLY 0.17 SQUARE MILES.

THE LARGEST CELL IN THE HUMAN BODY IS THE FEMALE EGG.

R2 D2, THE POPULAR ROBOT FROM THE *STAR WARS MOVIES*, IS CALLED C1 P8 IN THE ITALIAN MOVIE VERSIONS.

PAUL SIMON AND ART GARFUNKEL WERE CLASSMATES.

YOU CAN'T SNEEZE IN YOUR SLEEP.

THE ELEMENT CALIFORNIUM IS NAMED AFTER THE AMERICAN STATE, CALIFORNIA.

DUMDUM BULLETS ARE NAMED AFTER THE CITY WHERE THE AMMUNITION IS MANUFACTURED, DUMDUM, INDIA.

A SIFONAPTOROLOGIST STUDY FLEAS.

THE WEIGHT OF AN ADULT PERSON'S SKIN IS ABOUT 6.6 POUNDS.

TOM JONES PUT SO MUCH FEELING INTO A SONG HE RECORDED FOR THE JAMES BOND FILM *THUNDER BALL*, THAT HE BLACKED OUT IN THE STUDIO.

THE FIRST CERVICAL VERTEBRA ON HUMANS IS CALLED ATLAS.

VENUS, THE SECOND PLANET IN OUR SOLAR SYSTEM, ROTATES IN THE OPPOSITE DIRECTION OF THE OTHER EIGHT PLANETS.

IN THE BAHAMAS THERE ARE DIFFER-ENT CLASSIFICATIONS FOR STRONG WINDS. ONE IS "THE BANANA WIND" – THIS MEANS THE WIND IS SO STRONG, BANANAS ON THE TREES FALL TO THE GROUND.

PONT NEUF IS THE OLDEST
BRIDGE IN PARIS.

A LLAMA CAN SPIT 16.5 FEET.

A NORMAL HUMAN BRAIN CONTAINS
AS MANY BRAIN CELLS AS THERE
ARE STARS IN THE MILKY WAY;
ABOUT 100 MILLION.

THE THREADS IN NYLON STOCKINGS
ARE FIVE TIMES THINNER THAN
HUMAN HAIR.

OTHER SUGGESTED NAMES FOR THE
TV SERIES *MONY PYTHON'S FLYING
CIRCUS* WERE:
GWEN DIBLEY'S FLYING CIRCUS,
OWL-STRETCHING TIME,
*BUN, WHACKETT, BUZZARD, STUBBLE
AND BOOT,*
A TOAD ELEVATING MOMENT,
SEX AND VIOLENCE,
A HORSE, A BUCKET AND A SPOON.

THERE ARE OVER 500 RECOGNIZED
PHOBIAS. ONE OF THE MOST RARE
IS SCIOPHOBIA
– THE FEAR OF SHADOWS.

GERMS ARE VERY SMALL. ONE
SINGLE WATER DROPLET CAN
CONTAIN UP TO 50 MILLION GERMS.

THE ONLY VISIBLE HUMAN
MUSCLE IS THE TONGUE.

THERE IS A VERY UNUSUAL DIALECT
ON NEW GUINEA CALLED TAKI.
IT ONLY CONTAINS 340 WORDS.

DURING ONE SINGLE SOCCER MATCH, A PROFESSIONAL PLAYER CAN MOVE A DISTANCE OF 7 MILES.

GEORGE CLOONEY'S FIRST STARRING ROLE WAS A MINOR PART IN THE FILM *RETURN OF THE KILLER TOMATOES*.

CLEOPATRA COULD SPEAK 13 LANGUAGES.

THE ALBATROSS CAN
FLY WHILE SLEEPING.

THE NOTION OF COUNTING
BACKWARDS - AS DONE DURING A
SPACE ROCKET LAUNCH, FOR EXAM-
PLE – ORIGINATED FROM A GERMAN
SCIENCE FICTION FILM. THE DIRECTOR
THOUGHT THAT THE COUNTDOWN
WOULD INCREASE THE THRILL.

TAPEWORMS ARE CAPABLE OF GROW-
ING VERY LONG. THE LONGEST THAT
FAVOURS LIVING INSIDE HUMANS IS
THE TAENIA SAGINATA. FEMALES CAN
REACH UP TO 80-FEET.

THE WEAKEST MUSCLE IN THE HUMAN BODY IS THE STAPEDIUS MUSCLE WHICH IS LOCATED IN THE MIDDLE EAR. ITS ONLY FUNCTION IS TO MOVE THE 3 MILLIMETERS (1/8-INCH) STIRRUP BONE A 1/2-MILLIMETER (1/16-INCH).

KHMER IS THE WORLD'S LONGEST ALPHABET. IT CONTAINS 74 CHARACTERS AND IS USED BY ABOUT 8 MILLION PEOPLE IN CAMBODIA.

98% OF OUR GENES ARE THE SAME AS A CHIMPANZEES. ONLY 2% MAKE US A DIFFERENT SPECIES.

KISSING IS NOT ONLY NICE. IT'S ALSO GOOD FOR YOUR TEETH! IT'S BECAUSE WHEN YOU KISS, YOUR MOUTH PRODUCES SALIVA AND SALIVA HELPS PROTECT AGAINST DENTAL PLAQUE.

THE FOUR RINGS ON JELLYFISH ARE SEX ORGANS. THE MALE'S RINGS ARE WHITE ONES WHILE THE FEMALE ALSO HAS ADDITIONAL RED ONES.

OUR BLOOD CIRCULATION IS VERY LONG. THE BLOOD VESSELS, ALL TOGETHER, ARE BETWEEN 3,000 AND 6,000 MILES LONG.

A KOMODO DRAGON CAN EAT
ONE AND A HALF TIMES ITS OWN
BODY WEIGHT IN JUST A COUPLE
OF MINUTES.

MACH 1 IS THE TECHNICAL TERM
FOR THE SPEED OF SOUND – 742
MILES (STATUE) PER HOUR.

THE EARTH CIRCLES AROUND
THE SUN AT A SPEED OF
18.6 MILE PER SECOND.

A CONCORDE HOLDS 31,510 GALLONS OF PETROL IN ITS TANKS.

BEARS CAN BE LEFT OR RIGHT HANDED.

YOU SHARE THE SAME BIRTHDAY WITH ABOUT 9 MILLION OTHER PEOPLE.

THE WINGS ON A BANANA FLY FLAP BACK AND FORTH 200 TIMES PER SECOND.

120 MILLIGRAM OF ARSENIC
IS ENOUGH TO KILL YOU.

WHEN PHARMACIST JOHN PEMBER-
TON WAS MIXING THE SOLUTION
THAT LATER WAS TO BECOME
COCA-COLA, HE INCLUDED IN HIS
EXPERIENTAL BATCHES COCAINE,
COCA LEAVES AND COLA NUTS.

THELMA PICKLES WAS JOHN
LENNON'S FIRST GIRLFRIEND.

**WINSTON CHURCHILL WAS
BORN IN A LADIES LAVATORY.**

**THE CHAMELEON HAS A TONGUE
LONGER THAN ITS OWN BODY.**

**IN 1999; THE DANISH MOVIE *FESTEN*
RECEIVED A PECULIAR FILM AWARD
IN GERMANY FOR THE WORST
DUBBED MOVIE.**

IF YOU CUT A COCKROACH'S HEAD OFF, IT CAN LIVE FOR NINE MORE DAYS UNTIL IT STARVES TO DEATH.

THE ELECTRIC CHAIR WAS INVENTED BY A DENTIST.

DURING A FLIGHT, THE CONCORDE GETS 7 TO 8-INCHES LONGER. THE HEAT FROM THE FRICTION CAUSES THE METAL TO EXPAND.

THERE ARE MORE THAN 30,000
DIFFERENT KINDS OF ROSES.

THE GERMAN FRIEDRICH SERTÜNER,
WHEN HE MANAGED TO ISOLATE THE
ACTIVE SUBSTANCE FROM OPIUM
IN 1806, GAVE THE SUBSTANCE THE
NAME "MORPHINE" AFTER THE
GREEK GOD OF SLEEP.

THE KOALA BEAR IS LOVED BY
CHILDREN ALL OVER THE WORLD.
BUT DID YOU KNOW THAT IT´S ONE
OF THE SLEEPIEST ANIMALS IN THE
FAUNA? THE KOALA BEAR SPENDS
22 HOURS EVERY DAY SLEEPING.

THE SHORTEST KNOWN ALPHABET IS NEW GUINEA'S ROTOKAS. IT HAS ONLY 11 LETTERS –
A, B, E, G, I, K, O, P, R, T AND U.

DR. ALEXANDER WOODS INVENTED THE HYPODERMIC SYRINGE IN 1882.

IN JAPANESE, THE WORDS FOR "FOUR" AND "DEAD" ARE PRONOUNCED EXACTLY THE SAME. THIS IS ALSO TRUE FOR "NINE" AND "PAIN". THIS EXPLAINS WHY NO HOTEL ROOMS IN JAPAN HAVE THE NUMBERS 4 OR 9.

IF YOU FILL A CONE-SHAPED DRAM
GLASS HALFWAY, IT'S ACTUALLY
ONLY FILLED 12 – 13%.

HAVE YOU EVER TRIED TO LICK
YOUR OWN ELBOW? EVEN IF YOU
TRY, YOU WILL NEVER SUCCEED.
IT'S PHYSICALLY IMPOSSIBLE TO DO.

PHRENOLOGY IS AN OLD SCIENCE
THAT ADVOCATES THAT ONE CAN
UNDERSTAND THE CHARACTERISTICS
OF A PERSON BY THE SHAPE OF
THEIR SKULL.

THE AFRICAN OSTRICH LAYS THE LARGEST EGGS IN THE WORLD. THE SHELL IS 1.5 MILLIMETERS THICK AND IS STRONG ENOUGH TO HOLD THE WEIGHT OF AN ADULT MAN.

ANOTHER RARE PHOBIA IS LUTRAPHOBIA; – A DEATHLY FEAR OF OTTERS.

THE TALLEST PICASSO STATUE IN THE WORLD CAN BE FOUND IN KRISTINEHAMN, SWEDEN.

THE QUARTZ CRYSTAL IN A DIGITAL
WATCH VIBRATES 32,768 TIMES
EVERY SECOND.

STEVEN SPIELBERG DIDN'T ACCEPT
ANY MONEY FOR THE FILM
SCHINDLER'S LIST. HE FELT IT
WOULD BE BLOOD MONEY.

THE SEVEN BEAMS IN THE CROWN
OF THE STATUE OF LIBERTY
REPRESENT THE SEVEN SEAS
AND SEVEN CONTINENTS.

MONEY CONTAINS COTTON AS WELL AS PAPER. THAT'S WHY IT CAN SURVIVE A TUMBLE THROUGH THE WASHING MACHINE.

SHARKS ARE THE ONLY FISH THAT CAN BLINK BOTH EYES SIMULTANEOUSLY.

A SHARK'S SKELETON IS NOT MADE OF BONE LIKE OTHER FISH AND VERTEBRATES. INSTEAD, IT IS MADE-UP OF CARTILAGE.

THE ACTOR DOLPH LUNDGREN HAS A UNIVERSITY DEGREE FROM THE ROYAL TECHNICAL UNIVERSITY OF STOCKHOLM.

THE STEPPE PEOPLE IN CONGO, AFRICA, ARE THE TALLEST PEOPLE IN THE WORLD. MANY ARE 7 FEET TALL. THEY LIVE NEXT TO THE PYGMIES WHO ARE THE SHORTEST PEOPLE IN THE WORLD.

RHINOCEROS' HORNS ARE MADE UP OF COMPRESSED HAIR.

ORIGINALLY, COCA-COLA WAS SOLD AS A PRESCRIPTION TO CURE MELANCHOLY, HYSTERIA AND MIGRAINES.

THE SOHO AREA OF NEW YORK CITY IS NAMED SOHO BECAUSE IT IS LOCATED SOUTH OF HOUSTON STREET.

THE NATIONAL ANTHEM OF GREECE CONTAINS 158 VERSES.

THE PIG IS THE ONLY ANIMAL THAT, LIKE HUMANS, CAN GET A SUNTAN.

THE WORLD'S LONGEST CITY
NAME HAS 167 CHARACTERS.
KRUNGTHEPMAHANAKORNAMORNRAT-
TANAKOSINMAHINTARAYUTTHAYAMA-
HADILOKPHOPNOPARATR
JATHANIBURIROMUDOMRAJANIWESMA-
HASATHARNAMORNPHIMARNAVATARN-
SATHITSAKKATATTIYAVISANUKAMPRA-
SIT.
IT TRANSLATES INTO: THE GREAT CITY
OF ANGELS, THE SUPREME UNCONQUER-
ABLE LAND OF THE GREAT IMMORTAL
DIVINITY, THE ROYAL CAPITAL OF NINE
NOBLE GEMS, THE PLEASANT CITY, WITH
PLENTY OF GRAND ROYAL PALACES, AND
DIVINE PARADISES FOR THE REINCAR-
NATED DEITY, GIVEN BY INDRA AND CRE-
ATED BY THE GOD OF CRAFTING. IT IS
KNOWN TO THE REST OF THE WORLD AS
BANGKOK, THAILAND.

BRUCE WILLIS IS LEFT-HANDED. TO GET A BETTER CAMERA ANGLE, IN THE FILM SIXTH SENSE, HE WROTE WITH HIS RIGHT HAND IN ONE SCENE.

GRAMPUS, A PLAYFUL, BLACK AND WHITE DOLPHIN, CAN LIVE TO THE RIPE OLD AGE OF 80 TO 90 YEARS.

IT TAKES 240 MILLION YEARS FOR OUR SOLAR SYSTEM TO TRAVEL AROUND THE CENTRE OF OUR GALAXY, THE MILKY WAY. THIS IS KNOWN AS A COSMIC YEAR.

SOME OF THE LARGER BATTLE SCENES IN THE FILM *BRAVEHEART* HAD TO BE DONE TWICE, BECAUSE MANY PEOPLE WITH WALK-ON PARTS COULD BE SEEN WEARING WATCHES AND SUNGLASSES.

ANTOINE SAINT-EXPUÉRY, THE FRENCH AUTHOR WHO WROTE *THE LITTLE PRINCE*, DIED WHEN HIS SMALL PLANE CRASHED ON JULY 31, 1944. WHY THE PLANE CRASHED IS STILL UNKNOWN.

A MULE IS THE SPAWN OF A DONKEY AND A MARE.

COULFOPHOBIA IS THE TECHNICAL TERM FOR A FEAR OF CLOWNS.

***STAR TREK*, THE FAMOUS TV SERIES, WAS NOT A HIT WHEN IF FIRST STARTED. AFTER ONLY TWO SEASONS, THE TV STATION WANTED TO CANCEL IT.**

WRIGLEY'S, THE AMERICAN CHEWING GUM, WAS THE FIRST PRODUCT IN THE WORLD WITH A BAR CODE.

IF YOU SUFFER FROM POLYDACTYL,
YOU WERE BORN WITH MORE THAN
10 FINGERS AND TOES.

THE NOBEL PRIZEWINNER MARIE
CURIE WAS THE FIRST WOMAN
ALLOWED TO TEACH AT THE
UNIVERSITY OF SORBONNE IN PARIS.

A LIGHTNING BOLT WILL HEAT UP THE
AIR AROUND IT TO ABOUT 3,000°C
(5432 DEGREES FAHRENHEIT).

IN AN EARLIER VERSION OF THE SCRIPT FOR THE FILM *ALIEN*, RIPLEY WAS SUPPOSED TO BE PLAYED BY A MAN.

DURING THE FIRST WORLD WAR, JOSEF STALIN GOT OUT OF SERVING HIS MILITARY SERVICE BECAUSE OF HIS DEFORMED FEET. HE HAD TWO TOES THAT WERE GROWN TOGETHER.

A DRAGONFLY CAN FLY BACKWARDS AS FAST AS IT CAN FLY FORWARDS.

THE PITOHUIS, A GROUP OF BIRDS IN NEW GUINEA, HAVE POISONOUS FEATHERS AND SKIN. WHEN PREDATORS CATCH ONE OF THESE BIRDS, THEY INSTINCTIVELY SPIT IT OUT.

IF YOU LOVE COFFEE AND DRINK 100 CUPS IN FOUR HOURS, YOU WILL PROBABLY DIE FROM CAFFEINE POISONING.

BEFORE MICHAEL CAINE AND CHER CHANGED THEIR NAMES, THEY ANSWERED TO MAURICE MICKLEWHITE AND CHERILYN SARKISIAN LA PIERE.

ONLY TWO OF YOUR MOUTH MUSCLES
ARE REQUIRED FOR CREATING A
SMILE UNLESS YOU CONSIDER
THE MANY MUSCLES AROUND YOUR
EYES AS WELL.

MEN AND WOMEN BUTTON THEIR
SHIRTS DIFFERENTLY. A PRACTICE
THAT COMES FROM OLDEN TIMES
WHEN ROYAL MEN DRESSED
THEMSELVES BUT THE WOMEN USED
CHAMBERMAIDS WHO BUTTONED
THEIR BLOUSES FOR THEM FROM
THE FRONT.

THE LANGUAGE WITH THE GREATEST NUMBER OF WORDS IS ENGLISH. IT CONTAINS MORE THAN 455,000 ACTIVE WORDS AND 700,000 DEAD WORDS.

RAW ASPARAGUS IS SLIGHTLY POISONOUS.

ARNOLD SCHWARZENEGGER RECEIVED A COOL 15 MILLION DOLLARS FOR HIS PART IN *TERMINATOR 2*, WHERE HE ONLY SPOKE 700 WORDS. THAT'S $21,429 PER WORD. THE CLASSIC PHRASE "HASTA LA VISTA, BABY" EARNED HIM $85,716.

GHANDI'S FULL NAME WASN'T MAHATMA GANDHI.
HIS REAL NAME WAS MOHANDAS KARAMCHAND GANDHI. MAHATMA WAS A TITLE OF HONOUR WHICH MEANS LARGE SPIRIT.

THE TOOLS THAT WERE USED TO FIX UP JACK NAPIER (JACK NICHOLSON) AFTER HIS CHEMICAL BATH IN *BATMAN* ARE THE SAME TOOLS USED BY THE SADISTIC DENTIST, ORIN SCRIVELLO (STEVE MARTIN), IN THE 1986 FILM *LITTLE SHOP OF HORRORS*.

ON A FLIGHT FROM ANTWERP
TO LONDON IN 1997, 21 OF THE
PASSENGERS WERE 100 YEARS OLD.

MOST FISH STAY AWAKE MOST OF
THEIR LIVES. HOWEVER, THERE ARE
FISH THAT SLEEP. THEY LEAN
AGAINST A ROCK OR STAND
VERTICALLY IN THE WATER.

A SNAIL CAN SLEEP
FOR THREE YEARS.

MOSQUITOES CAN TRACK PEOPLE UP TO 110 YARDS AWAY BY THE SUBSTANCES IN THEIR BREATH.

THE LARGEST PAINTING IN THE WORLD IS *THE BATTLE AT GETTYS-BURG*, CREATED BY THE AMERICAN PAUL PHILLIPOTEAUX AND 16 OF HIS ASSISTANTS. IT STANDS 68.8-FEET HIGH AND IS 410-FEET WIDE.

THE TYRANNOSAURUS REX SUFFERED FROM GOUT.

**THERE ARE 336 CAVITIES
IN A GOLF BALL.**

**THE MOST WIDELY USED LANGUAGE
IN THE WORLD IS MANDARIN-CHI-
NESE, THE MOTHER TONGUE FOR
ALMOST 900 MILLION PEOPLE. ONLY
332 MILLION PEOPLE HAVE ENGLISH
AS THEIR MOTHER TONGUE.**

**TO PRODUCE 1 SINGLE GRAM OF
SERUM, YOU NEED POISON
FROM 150 COBRA BITES.**

ALFRED NOBEL'S BROTHER EMIL,
DIED IN AN EXPLOSION IN THE
LABORATORY WHERE BOTH BROTHERS
WERE PERFORMING EXPERIMENTS
WITH EXPLOSIVE OILS, THE
FORERUNNER TO DYNAMITE.

IF ALL THE RAIN IN OUR ATMOSPHERE
FELL AT THE SAME TIME, IT WOULD
COVER THE EARTH WITH A ONE-INCH
THICK LAYER OF WATER.

THE CENTRE OF THE SUN IS 15
MILLION DEGREES CELCIUS.
THE SURFACE IS ONLY 5,800 DEGREES
CELCIUS (10472 DEGREES
FAHRENHEIT).

THE SALT IN YOUR TEARS COMES FROM THE FOOD YOU EAT. IT´S TRANSPORTED VIA THE BLOOD CIRCULATION TO THE LACRIMAL GLAND NEAR YOUR EYES WHERE TEARS ARE PRODUCED.

IF YOU SUFFER FROM DENTOPHOBIA, YOU HAVE AN EXTREME FEAR OF DENTISTS.

JONATHAN FRAKES REFUSED TO SHAVE HIS BACK IN THE LOVE SCENE WITH MARTINA MARTIS IN THE FILM *STAR TREK: NEMESIS*. THE HAIR HAD TO BE DIGITALLY REMOVED.

THE BLACK LINES, ON A BAR CODE,
SYMBOLIZE THE FIGURE 1 AND THE
WHITE LINES SYMBOLIZE THE FIGURE
2. TOGETHER THEY FORM A LONG
CODE THAT CONTAINS ALL
NECESSARY DATA ON A PRODUCT.

THE BIGGEST DIFFERENCE BETWEEN
AN "EBB" AND A "FLOOD" WAS
MEASURED IN NOVA SCOTIA,
CANADA'S BAY OF FUNDY.
THE DIFFERENCE WAS 52 FEET.

ICHTHYOSAURS, SEA DWELLING DINOSAURS, LIVED DURING THE JURASIC PERIOD AND HAD EYES 9-INCHES WIDE.

THE PINK OR RED COLOUR ON FLAMINGOS INDICATES THAT THE BIRD HAS BECOME SEXUALLY MATURE. THEY´RE WHITE WHEN THEY ARE BORN BUT AFTER A YEAR THEY GET THEIR COLOUR.

**BARBIE'S FULL NAME IS
BARBARA MILLICENT ROBERTS.**

**THE SONG OF A HUMPBACK WHALE
CAN REACH 190 DB. THAT'S
EQUIVALENT TO THE SOUND OF
A BOEING 747 AT TAKEOFF.**

**BEFORE JOSEF STALIN BECAME A
REVOLUTIONIST, HE CONSIDERED
A CAREER AS A PRIEST. HE WAS
THROWN OUT OF SEMINARY,
THOUGH, BECAUSE OF HIS DRINKING
AND AGGRESSIVE BEHAVIOUR.**

WALT DISNEY WAS AFRAID OF MICE.

TWENTY PERCENT OF THE WORLD'S POPULATION HAS A GENETIC DISOR-DER THAT CAUSES THE LACK OF WISDOM TEETH.

COCO WATER, THE FLUID IN YOUNG, TINY COCONUTS, CAN BE USED AS A SUBSTITUTE FOR BLOOD PLASMA.

**THE LARGEST KNOWN SHARK IS
THE GREAT WHITE SHARK.
IT CAN BECOME 46 FEET LONG.**

**THE AVERAGE CAR STANDS
STILL 23 HOURS OF THE DAY.**

**50% OF ALL BANK ROBBERIES
ARE DONE ON FRIDAYS.**

**200 CHILDREN ARE BORN
EVERY MINUTE.**

ALEXANDER GRAHAM BELL, WHO
INVENTED THE TELEPHONE, COULD
NEVER TALK TO HIS MOTHER OR
WIFE ON IT. THEY WERE BOTH DEAF.

ALFRED HITCHCOCK HAD
NO BELLY BUTTON.

A SHRIMP'S HEART IS
LOCATED IN ITS HEAD.

IN AN 80 YEAR LONG STUDY ON
200,000 OSTRICHES,
NOT A SINGLE CASE WAS REPORTED
WHERE AN OSTRICH BURIED ITS HEAD
IN THE GROUND.

IT IS PHYSICALLY IMPOSSIBLE FOR
A PIG TO LOOK UP AT THE SKY.

MORE THAN 50% OF THE WORLD'S
POPULATION HAVE NEVER MADE
OR RECEIVED A TELEPHONE CALL.

HORSES CAN'T THROW UP.

THE MOST DIFFICULT WORDS TO SAY FAST IN ENGLISH ARE "SIXTH SICK SHEIK'S SIXTH SHEEP'S SICK".

RATS CAN BREED SO FAST THAT AFTER ONLY EIGHTEEN MONTHS THEY CAN PRODUCE MORE THAN A MILLION OFF-SPRING.

IF YOU USE EAR PHONES FOR ONE HOUR, YOU WILL INCREASE THE AMOUNT OF BACTERIA IN YOUR EARS BY 700%.

23% OF ALL COPY MACHINE BREAK-DOWNS COME FROM PEOPLE SITTING ON THEM TO MAKE COPIES OF THEIR OWN BUTTS.

NEARLY ALL LIPSTICKS CONTAIN FISH SCALES.

NO PAPER CAN BE FOLDED IN
HALF MORE THAN 7 TIMES.

IN ONE YEAR, AMERICAN AIRLINES
SAVED $40,000 BY DECREASING THE
NUMBER OF OLIVES BY JUST ONE ON
EACH FIRST-CLASS SALAD.

YOU BURN MORE CALORIES
SLEEPING THAN WATCHING TV.

THE KING OF HEARTS IS THE ONLY
KING WITHOUT A MOUSTACHE.

MOST OF THE DUST IN YOUR
HOME COMES FROM YOUR OWN
DEAD SKIN CELLS.

IN ONE YEAR BASKETBALL ICON,
MICHAEL JORDAN, EARNED MORE
MONEY FROM HIS SPONSOR, NIKI,
THAN ALL OF THE EMPLOYEES PUT
TOGETHER AT THE MALAYSIA NIKI
FACTORY.

RICHARD MILLHOUSE NIXON WAS THE FIRST AMERICAN PRESIDENT WHOSE NAME INCLUDED ALL THE LETTERS IN THE WORD "CRIMINAL".

TURTLES CAN BREATHE THROUGH THEIR BUTTS.

ACCORDING TO THE OXFORD ENGLISH DICTIONARY, THE LONGEST ENGLISH WORD IS PNEUMONOULTRAMICRO-SCOPICSILICOVOLCANOKONIOSIS. THE FORTY-FIVE-LETTER WORD IS THE NAME OF A SPECIAL FORM OF SILICOSIS CAUSED BY ULTRAMICRO-SCOPIC PARTICLES OF SILICA VOLCANIC DUST...

INGROWN NAILS ARE HEREDITARY.

THE LONGEST GEOGRAPHICAL NAME
STILL IN USE IS THE NAME OF A HILL
IN NEW ZEELAND. IT'S CALLED
TAUMATAWHAKATANGIHA
NGAKOAUAUOTAMATEATURIPUKAKA-
PIKIMAUNGAHORONUKUPOKAIWE
NUAKIT NATAHU.

TELLY SAVALAS AND LOUIS
ARMSTRONG BOTH DIED ON
THEIR BIRTHDAYS.

DONALD DUCK'S MIDDLE
NAME IS FAUNTLEROY.

THE INITIALS FOR THE RUSSIAN
SECRET SERVICE "KGB" STAND FOR
KOMITET GOSUDARSTVENNOY
BEZOPASNOSTI.

THE KANGAROO AND EMU CAN'T
MOVE BACKWARDS. THAT'S WHY
THEY HAVE BEEN CHOSEN AS
SYMBOLS FOR THE AUSTRALIAN
CONTINENT.

GORDON SUMNER, THE ROCK STAR ALSO KNOWN AS STING, GOT HIS NICKNAME FROM THE YELLOW-BLACK T-SHIRTS HE USED TO WEAR. THE OTHER BAND MEMBERS THOUGHT HE LOOKED LIKE A BUMBLEBEE.

TASTE BUDS ONLY LIVE FOR 10 DAYS.

UNTIL 1890, THE CHOIR BOYS IN THE VATICAN WERE CASTRATED TO PREVENT THEIR VOICES FROM BECOMING DEEPER.

RESEARCH SHOWS MOSQUITOES LIKE PEOPLE WHOM HAVE RECENTLY EATEN BANANAS.

A CAT HAS A LARGER CHANCE OF SURVIVING A FALL FROM THE 20TH FLOOR THAN FROM THE 7TH FLOOR.

IF NASA DECIDED TO SEND BIRDS UP IN SPACE, THE BIRDS WOULD SOON DIE. THEY NEED GRAVITY TO SWALLOW.

EVERY TIME YOU LICK A STAMP, YOU WILL EAT ONE TENTH OF A CALORIE.

ON AVERAGE, AN ADULT LAUGHS 15 TIMES A DAY WHILE A BABY LAUGHS 400 TIMES A DAY.

111,111,111 X 111,111,111 = 12,345,678,987,654,321

ONE LEG OF A DOVE WEIGHS LESS
THAT ITS FEATHERS.

YOUR HEARING IS BETTER WHEN YOU
ARE HUNGRY THAN WHEN YOU'VE
JUST EATEN.

THE MOST COMMON REPORTED
TIME TO SEE A UFO IS AT 2300
HOURS (11 PM).

**THERE ARE 31,557,600
SECONDS IN A YEAR.**

**IF A SQUID IS EXTREMELY HUNGRY,
IT CAN EAT ITS OWN ARMS.**

**THE GREATEST AMOUNT OF BACTERIA
ON YOUR BODY IS HIDDEN BETWEEN
YOUR TOES.**

**DID YOU KNOW THAT THE YO-YO IS
THE OLDEST TOY, AFTER THE DOLL?**

THE WORD "WAR" IN SANSKRIT
MEANS "WISH FOR MORE COWS".

KANGAROOS ARE
LACTOSE INTOLERANT.

ACCORDING TO THE LAW OF
MASSACHUSETTS, GOATS ARE
NOT ALLOWED TO WEAR PANTS.

THIS YEAR YOU WILL BLOW YOUR NOSE 250 TIMES.

MOSQUITOES HAVE 47 TEETH.

IN THE CITY OF LAWRENCE, KANSAS, IT'S AGAINST THE LAW TO WALK AROUND WITH BEES IN YOUR HAT.

ONLY 30% OF ALL HUMAN BEINGS
CAN FLARE THEIR NOSTRILS.

MORE THAN 250 PEOPLE HAVE
FALLEN FROM THE LEANING TOWER
OF PISA SINCE THE YEAR 1174.

IN ANCIENT EGYPT,
THE PENALTY FOR KILLING
A CAT WAS DEATH.

ACCORDING TO AN 1845 BRITISH LAW
- IF YOU ATTEMPTED TO COMMIT
SUICIDE, YOU WERE SENTENCED
TO DEATH.

ONCE UPON A TIME, CHRISTMAS WAS
FORBIDDEN IN ENGLAND.

IN HARTFORD, CONNECTICUT YOU ARE
NOT ALLOWED TO KISS YOUR WIFE
ON SUNDAYS.

IN KENTUCKY, IT'S AGAINST THE LAW
TO WALK AROUND WITH ICE CREAM
IN YOUR HIP POCKET.

SINCE 1916, WHEN A MAN MAILED A
40,000 TON BRICK HOUSE IN ORDER
TO AVOID HIGH FREIGHT COSTS, IT IS
FORBIDDEN TO SEND A WHOLE BUILD-
ING BY MAIL IN THE UNITED STATES.

A FULLY LOADED OIL TANKER
NEEDS 20 MINUTES TO STOP.

ALL SUNLIGHT THAT HITS THE
SURFACE OF THE EARTH DURING ANY
GIVEN MOMENT, WEIGHS AS MUCH
AS A CRUISE SHIP.

WHEN THE ATOMIC BOMB WAS
DEVELOPED IN THE AMERICAN CITY
OF ALAMOGORDO, NEW MEXICO, THE
MILITARY BASE PREFERRED STAFF
THAT WERE ILLITERATE AS THE
AUTHORITIES DIDN'T WANT THE RISK
OF HAVING WORKERS THAT COULD
READ CONFIDENTIAL PAPERS FROM
THE WASTE BINS.

EVERY YEAR, 4,000 PEOPLE ARE
INJURED BY TEA POTS.

ALL HOSPITALS IN SINGAPORE
USE PAMPERS DIAPERS.

COLGATE HAD A BIG CHALLENGE
WHEN THEY RELEASED THEIR TOOTH
PASTE IN SPANISH SPEAKING
COUNTRIES. COLGATE MEANS
"GO HANG YOURSELF" IN SPANISH.

ON AVERAGE, THERE ARE 333 PIECES OF TOILET PAPER ON ONE TOILET ROLL.

YOUR BODY CONTAINS ABOUT 100,000,000,000,000 CELLS.

NO AMERICAN PRESIDENT HAS HAD BROWN EYES.

**THE ONLY PART OF YOUR BODY
THAT CAN'T GET CANCER,
IS THE LENS OF THE EYE.**

**FEMALE HYENAS HAVE
UNDERDEVELOPED PENISES.**

**THE DISTANCE BETWEEN THE
SURFACE AND THE CENTRE OF THE
EARTH IS 3,700 MILES.**

**BOWLING WAS INVENTED
IN EGYPT 5,000 B.C.**

**DALMATIANS ARE BORN
WITHOUT SPOTS.**

**DOLPHINS ALWAYS KEEP ONE
EYE OPEN WHILE SLEEPING.**

EUROPE AND NORTH AMERICA ARE DRIFTING APART AT THE SAME SPEED IT TAKES OUR NAILS TO GROW.

LEONARDO DA VINCI COULD WRITE WITH ONE HAND AND PAINT WITH THE OTHER – SIMULTANEOUSLY.

THERE ARE NO CLOCKS IN LAS VEGAS CASINOS.

THE HOTTEST PLACE ON EARTH
IS EL AZIZIA IN LIBYA.

RIGHT-HANDED PEOPLE LIVE APPROX-
IMATELY 9 YEARS LONGER THAN
LEFT-HANDED PEOPLE.

IN ONE YEAR,
MORE MONOPOLY MONEY
IS PRINTED THAN REAL MONEY.

EVERY CHOCOLATE BAR PRODUCED
CONTAINS AN AVERAGE OF
8 INSECT LEGS.

A POLAR BEAR'S SKIN IS BLACK.

ELVIS HAD A TWIN BROTHER
WHO DIED AT BIRTH. HIS
NAME WAS GARON.

IN CHINA, THERE ARE MORE PEOPLE WHO SPEAK ENGLISH THAN IN THE USA.

IF ALL THE INHABITANTS OF CHINA WALKED PASSED YOU IN A SINGLE LINE, THE LINE WOULD NEVER STOP IF YOU TAKE INTO CONSIDERATION THE RATE OF REPRODUCTION.

ANTS ALWAYS FALL ON THEIR RIGHT SIDE IF THEY GET DRUNK.

IF YOU SELL EVERY USEFUL PART
OF YOUR BODY, YOU WILL GET
$35 MILLION.

THE WORLD RECORD FOR AN
UNDERWATER KISS IS 2 MINUTES
AND 18 SECONDS.

5% OF ALL ADULTS SLEEPWALK.

A GOOD BUTLER SHOULD CHANGE SHOES EVERY THREE HOURS.

ADOLF HITLER'S FAVOURITE MOVIE WAS *KING KONG*.

IT WOULD TAKE 1.12 MILLION MOSQUITOES, STINGING YOU ALL AT THE SAME TIME, TO COMPLETELY EMPTY YOUR BODY OF ITS BLOOD.

ONE OF THE REASONS FIDEL CASTRO GREW A BEARD WAS THAT THE EMBARGOES FROM THE USA MADE IT DIFFICULT TO GET RAZOR BLADES.

IT TAKES AN ADULT ABOUT 138 MINUTES TO WATCH *BRIDGES OVER MADISON COUNTY* BUT ONLY 118 MINUTES TO READ THE BOOK.

THE GLUE ON STAMPS IN ISRAEL IS KOSHER APPROVED.

"DNA" STANDS FOR
DEOXYRIBONUCLEIC ACID.

THE SCIENTIFIC WORD FOR
PICKING ONE'S NOSE IS
RHINOTILLEXONAMIA.

SYLVESTER STALLONE ONCE WORKED
IN A CIRCUS CLEANING LION CAGES.

MICHAEL JACKSON'S SONG *BILLY JEAN* WAS THE FIRST MUSICAL VIDEO SHOWN ON MTV THAT WAS MADE BY AN AFRICAN-AMERICAN PERFORMER.

AN AIRPORT IN ENGLAND USES SONGS BY TINA TURNER TO SCARE BIRDS OFF THE RUNWAY.

IN 1938, ADOLF HITLER WAS ELECTED *TIMES* MAGAZINE'S "MAN OF THE YEAR".

WHEN ALBERT EINSTEIN DIED,
HIS BRAIN WAS PUT IN A JAR TO
BE EXAMINED AND SAVED FOR
THE FUTURE.

IN 1978, EMILIO MARCO PALMA WAS
THE FIRST PERSON TO BE BORN IN
THE ANTARCTIC.

ON AVERAGE 7.5% OF ALL OFFICE
DOCUMENTS DISAPPEAR.

BILL GATES BEGAN PROGRAMMING
COMPUTERS WHEN HE WAS
13 YEARS OLD.

IN THE USA, YOUNG PEOPLE BUY
$40 MILLION DOLLARS' WORTH
OF CHEWING GUM EVERY YEAR.

NEARLY EVERY PHOTO ADVERTISING
A WATCH SHOWS THE TIME TO BE
10:10 AM.

SINGLE PEOPLE ARE SEVEN AND
A HALF TIMES MORE LIKELY TO
REQUIRE PSYCHIATRIC CARE.

DURING A LIFETIME, YOU WILL
PRODUCE ENOUGH SALIVA TO FILL
UP TWO SWIMMING POOLS.

IN AVERAGE, A FOUR YEAR OLD
CHILD WILL ASK 437 QUESTIONS
EVERY DAY.

NOBODY KNOWS WHY, BUT 90% OF ALL WOMEN WALK DIRECTLY TO THE RIGHT WHEN THEY ENTER A DEPARTMENT STORE.

IN NEW YORK, 311 PERSONS GET BITTEN BY RATS EVERY YEAR. 1519 PERSONS ARE BITTEN BY OTHER NEW YORKERS.

IF A FLEA WAS A HUMAN BEING, IT WOULD BE ABLE TO JUMP 1000 FEET STRAIGHT UP IN THE AIR.

MORE THAN TWO-THIRDS OF ALL PEOPLE, WHO HAVE REACHED 65 OR OLDER, ARE STILL LIVING.

YOU WILL INHALE ABOUT 44 POUNDS OF DUST DURING YOUR LIFE.

BABIES ARE ALWAYS BORN WITH BLUE EYES.

MORE THAN 8,000 NON-FUNCTIONING SATELLITES ARE CIRCLING AROUND THE EARTH.

IN 1988, A POODLE FELL FROM A HIGH-RISE BUILDING IN BUENOS AIRES AND KILLED THREE PEOPLE. ONE GOT THE POODLE ON HIS HEAD, A BUS HIT THE OTHER AND THE THIRD HAD A HEART ATTACK, WATCHING IT ALL.

BILL WYMAN, FORMER BASS GUITARIST FOR *THE ROLLING STONES*, DATED MANDY SMITH, WHOM HE LATER MARRIED, WHEN SHE WAS ONLY THIRTEEN. SEVEN YEARS LATER STEPHEN, WYMAN'S SON, MARRIED MANDY'S MOTHER. THIS MAKES STEPHEN A STEPFATHER TO HIS OWN STEPMOTHER.

UNSOLVED MYSTERIES

IF YOU ATTEMPT TO FAIL AND SUCCEED, WHAT HAVE YOU REALLY DONE?

WHY IS TIME WHEN TRAFFIC MOVES SLOWLY, CALLED RUSH HOUR?

HOW FAST IS THE SPEED OF DARK?

IF BARBIE IS SO POPULAR, WHY DO YOU HAVE TO BUY HER FRIENDS?

**WHAT HAPPENS IF YOU ARE
SCARED HALF TO DEATH, TWICE?**

**HOW CAN A HOUSE BURN UP
WHEN IT'S BURNING DOWN?**

**IF YOUR VACUUM CLEANER SUCKS,
IS THAT A BAD THING?**

**HOW CAN YOU TELL IF A SMURF IS
CHOKING ON SOMETHING?**

IF A WORD IN THE DICTIONARY
IS MISSPELLED. HOW WOULD
YOU KNOW IT?

IF YOU EXPECT THE UNEXPECTED,
IS THE UNEXPECTED THEN EXPECTED?

IF YOU TAKE A PICTURE OF CHEESE,
WHAT DOES IT SAY?

DOES A TEA DRINKER
HAVE COFFEE BREAKES?

WHY DO THEY REPORT
POWER OUTAGES ON TV?

WHY DO YOU PRESS HARDER ON THE
REMOTE CONTROL BUTTONS WHEN
THE BATTERIES ARE DEAD?

IF IT´S +-0 DEGREES CELSIUS IN THE EVENING AND IT WILL BE TWICE AS COLD THE NEXT MORNING, HOW COLD WILL IT THEN BE?

WHY IS THE WORD "ABBREVIATION" SO LONG?

HOW COME A MAN CAN BELIEVE THAT THERE ARE 400 BILLION STARS, BUT IF YOU TELL HIM THAT THE PAINT IS WET, HE´S GONNA GO AHEAD AND TOUCH IT?

HOW COULD SOMEONE BE SO CRUEL TO PUT AN "S" IN THE WORD "LISP"?

WOULD A FLY WITHOUT WINGS BE CALLED A WALK?

WHY DOES YOUR HAIR TURN LIGHT IN THE SUN WHEN YOUR SKIN GETS DARKER?

WHY CAN'T GIRLS PUT THEIR MASCARA ON WITH THEIR MOUTH CLOSED?

HOW COME YOU NEVER SEE THE
HEADLINE "PSYCHIC WOMAN
WINS LOTTERY"?

IN WINDOWS 98, HOW COME YOU
HAVE TO PRESS THE "START"
BUTTON TO TURN THE
COMPUTER OFF?

WHY ISN'T THERE MOUSE
FLAVOURED CAT FOOD?

WHEN DOG FOOD HAS A "NEW AND
IMPROVED TASTE", WHO TASTED IT?

IF THE BLACK BOX IN AIRPLANES IS
UNBREAKABLE, WHEN THEN DON'T
THEY BUILD THE WHOLE PLANE IN
THAT MATERIAL?

WHY DON'T SHEEP SHRINK
WHEN IT RAINS?

IF IT'S SO SAFE TO FLY, WHY IS THE
AIRPORT CALLED "TERMINAL"?

WHEN GIVING A LETHAL INJECTION IN
AN AMERICAN PRISON, WHY IS THE
NEEDLE FIRST STERILIZED?

WHAT HAPPENS IF YOU TRAVEL AT THE SPEED OF LIGHT, THEN TURN YOUR HEADLIGHTS ON?

ARE THERE HUMAN GUIDES FOR BLIND DOGS?

WHAT IS A FREE GIFT?

IF A SCHIZOPHRENIC PERSON THREATENS TO KILL HIMSELF, IS THAT CONSIDERED A HOSTAGE SITUATION?

IF YOU END UP IN A LIFE CRISIS
WHILE PLAYING HIDE AND SEEK,
DO YOU AUTOMATICALLY LOOSE
BECAUSE YOU CAN'T FIND
YOURSELF?

WHO TOWS THE TOW TRUCK
WHEN IT BREAKS DOWN?

IF OLIVE OIL COMES FROM OLIVES,
THEN WHERE DOES BABY OIL
COME FROM?

ANOTHER WORD FOR SYNONYM?

WHY IS IT CALLED MISSILE? SHOULDN'T IT BE CALLED HITTILE INSTEAD?

DOES WATER FLOAT?

WHAT HAPPENS TO THE WHITE WHEN THE SNOW MELTS?

WHY IS A BOXING RING SQUARE?

WHY DO PEOPLE SCREAM "HEADS UP!" WHEN SOMETHING IS COMING TOWARDS YOU? DO THEY WANT YOU TO GET IT IN YOUR FACE?

WHY DOESN'T GLUE STICK TO THE INSIDE OF THE BOTTLE

IF YOU PLANT BIRD SEED?

CONFESSIONS
Shameful Secrets of Everyday People
91-974396-6-5
Humor
March 2005

Eavesdropping in the Confessional

Like being a fly on the wall in any church confessional, these incredible real online admissions of people's darkest secrets are alternately disturbing, whimsical and hilarious. Sure to spark interesting conversations, this is the perfect therapeutic gift to share with friends and loved ones (and perhaps detested enemies, with certain confessions circled in red and "I know your secret" handwritten nearby).

Dirty MovieQuoteBook
91-974396-9-X
Humor/Film
May 2005

Saucy Sayings of Cinema

With over 700 saucy, sexy quotes from the funniest and most sordid films ever produced. A movie quiz game in a book. An excellent source of fresh pick-up or put-down lines, this titillating guide is sure to put anyone in the mood for love.

Cult MovieQuoteBook
91-974396-3-0
Humor/Film
May 2005

A Film Buff's Dictionary of Classic Lines

Over 700 memorable, provocative, hilarious and thought- provoking quotes fill this fascinating guide, a kind of dictionary for movie quote buffs. Going beyond the old standards such as "Here's Looking at You Kid," this handbook pulls quotes from a surprisingly eclectic variety of global cinematic gems, and will have even the most diehard movie buffs frantic to place the line with the film.

The World´s Coolest Baby Names
91-974883-1-3
Pop Culture
July 2005

A Name Book for the 21st Century Parent

A perfect name guide to spice up any baby shower name game.
Baby names aren't handed down anymore, and the coolest names are as much from pop culture as from the Bible. Hybrid names from popular and arcane sources in literature, television, and film create some very memorable name combinations. Includes the amusing trivia behind the names' origins and is sure to spark scads of arguments in expectant families everywhere!

Gordon Gecko - Wallstreet - Kissy Suzuki - you only live twice - Bobby Peru - wild at heart - Holly Golightly - breakfast at tiffany´s - Alexander de Large - a clock work orange - Phoebe Buffay - friends

The Pet Cookbook
Have your best friend for dinner
91-974883-4-8
Humor/Cooking
July 2005

Domesticated Delicacies from Around the World

On a global scale, one man's pet is another man's supper, and this wild
cookbook shares the best recipes from around the world on how to
prepare those delectable little dishes from the domesticated animal kingdom.
Scorpion Soup with a Sting, Pony 'n' Pepperoni Pizza, Parrot Piroge, and
Goldfish Tortilla Wrap are just a few samples of the eclectic world cuisine
within. Decidedly not for vegetarians.

*No animals were hurt during the making of this book.

    SCORPION SOUP WITH A STING
    CREAMY PARAKEET PASTA
    PARROT PIROGE
    GUINEA PIG PIE
    GOLDFISH TORTILLA WRAP
    MUD TURTLE RISOTTO